A Heart for Others

Learning to Model
The Witnessing Style
Of Jesus

Andrew Jackson

YWAM Publishing
A Ministry of Youth With A Mission
P.O. Box 55787, Seattle, WA 98155

Dedication

With a grateful heart to Floyd McClung, Jr.
—my friend and mentor.

With gratitude....

I express my deepest appreciation for the support and encouragement of everyone at YWAM Publishing; my church family at Kempsville Presbyterian Church; and especially to my wife Barbara, whose heart for others surpasses anyone I know; and to our children, Rachael, Luke, and Sarah Grace, whom I love beyond measure.

Foreword

I first met Andy Jackson almost 20 years ago. Andy became a Christian through an evangelistic ministry called The Ark, which I was leading in the city of Amsterdam. From a scraggly young world traveler, Andy has grown to be a mature disciple of Christ and now pastors a large Evangelical Presbyterian Church.

I have followed Andy's growth as a Christian and his development as a leader in the Body of Christ. He has a passion for the world and is deeply committed to equipping Christians to share their faith personally and effectively.

Andy's book is the kind that every believer will enjoy reading. He does not heap guilt upon us or try to motivate us with pious phrases.

Andy Jackson identifies the key issues we all face in sharing our faith:

- Should I witness or should I wait?

- How do I overcome my fears without becoming a fool?

- How do I open up a conversation without becoming mechanical?

- How do I cultivate a compassion for people in the midst of the pressures and busyness of life?

Andy Jackson reminds us that while .5 percent of all believers come to the Lord through evangelistic crusades, 75 percent are led to the Lord by a friend or relative. The greatest evangelists in the world are not famous; they are ordinary Christians who struggle with real-life issues, and in spite of their weaknesses, reach out to friends and relatives in need. The greatest evangelists in the world do not stand on platforms, but get involved in the lives of their friends.

I recommend this book as a study guide for small groups and home fellowships. Sunday school teachers will find it a great aid in teaching classes on evangelism.

I trust it will be as great a help to you as it has been to me in motivating me to step across the line separating those who desire to be wise from those who are afraid to speak up. That is the difference between fear and faith, between obedience and copping out.

—Floyd McClung, Jr.

Table of Contents

*Whoever claims to live in
him must walk as Jesus did.*

I John 2:6

Introduction

If you spent time in Seattle during the early 1970s, you may remember as vividly as I do a man standing on a busy downtown street corner. He called out in a droning monotone to people passing by, "You'll be cast into an eternal lake of fire from which there's no escape. You must repent! You're on your way to hell. You could die today! Repent now! Stand with me. Confess your sins."

Like many others, I invariably found some excuse to cross the street about the time this man came within earshot. Those who had the misfortune to get trapped on his side of the street either began rummaging through their bags or developed a fascination with their shoelaces as they walked by. I never once saw anyone who even appeared to notice this street preacher, much less who stopped to listen to him or who stood with him and confessed their sins.

I was not a Christian then, and this man's witnessing approach repulsed me. Even now I find myself flinching inside as I recall his method. The man's message may have been theologically sound, but his method of communication failed miserably. Instead of communicating God's love effectively and drawing people to Jesus Christ, his message repelled most of them. What is even more disturbing is that this man didn't seem to notice how unfruitful and obnoxious his method of witnessing was. He had a life-changing message to give to people, but he shared it in a way that only brought scorn and ridicule.

Many of you can identify with my experience. Perhaps you have felt repulsed when you encountered a person who shared the Gospel in an inappropriate way. Or maybe you're aware that you also have a life-changing message to share, but somehow your best attempts seem to fall short. Don't throw in the towel! This book was written especially with you in mind.

The Gospels record an instance where Jesus used Simon Peter's fishing boat as a platform from which to preach (Luke 5:1-11). When Jesus was finished preaching, He instructed Peter to take the boat farther from the shore and let down his nets for a catch. "Master," Peter responded, "we've worked hard all night and haven't caught anything. But because you say so, I will let down the nets."

We all know how the story goes. Peter obediently let down his nets, and caught so many fish that his boat was in danger of sinking. Peter had to call for his partners, James and John, to help him with the load. When they finally returned to the shore, Jesus challenged them, "Don't be afraid; from now on you will catch men." Luke goes on to tell us, "So they pulled their boats up on shore, left everything and followed him...."

It is interesting that immediately after they had caught a large number of fish, Jesus promised them that they would also "catch" men. The theological implication was that if they left their nets and followed Him, Jesus would teach them to "catch" as many people as they had caught fish.

As Christ's followers, we are also called to be fishers of men. We are called first to *tell* people that there is hope, forgiveness, and freedom in the Lord Jesus Christ, and that if they invite Him into their lives, He will radically change them forever. Second, we are to *teach* them how to apply the Gospel to their daily lives. That is what Jesus meant by "catching" men. The question then arises, "Is that what we're doing? Are we witnessing effectively to men and women and drawing them into the Kingdom of God?"

I pastor a large church, and I constantly ask these questions of myself and of our church. I know from experience that it is easy to exert a lot of personal and corporate energy pursuing and developing evangelism strategies ranging from door-to-door witnessing campaigns to large evangelistic rallies. I have noticed that it is easy to become enamored with the mechanics and techniques of witnessing programs which can quickly take on a life of their own.

Unfortunately, witnessing activity does not necessarily produce results. After all, our ultimate goal is *changed lives*, not a large number on a tally sheet of doors we've knocked on. My firsthand experience with institutionalized witnessing programs has taught me that they usually produce few measurable results while absorbing large amounts of the church's energy and resources.

I recently read a poignant story which emphasized this fact. A pastor who was totally committed to a door-to-door evangelism program shared that, after a year, those involved with the program in his church had knocked on 4,000 doors. It was an effort of which the pastor was very proud. But when he was asked how many people had given their lives to the Lord Jesus as a result, the pastor's answer was very revealing: "None"! When the pastor was asked about the church's lack of results and his response, he answered, "Why, next year we'll double our efforts and knock on 8,000 doors."

This pastor's reply is tragic. To him witnessing was a program of door-knocking and scripted monologues. He thought that if his church members applied enough effort and knocked on enough doors, eventually they would win someone to the Lord Jesus. It never occurred to him to question the program's effectiveness. Rather, he perceived that a redoubling of their efforts would produce the desired results.

It seems self-evident that we should prayerfully evaluate everything we do in light of its effectiveness. When we evaluate the spiritual effectiveness of our lives, many of us discover that we are bound to "traditional" ways of witnessing. Unfortunately, many of these methods are unhelpful and unproductive. Some of these techniques may have worked well in other situations or at other times. Some of us may still use them with limited results. However, we need to set aside our preconceived notions and hold all that we do—both individually and corporately—to the light and scrutiny of Scripture and the test of spiritual fruitfulness. God's will is that we bear much fruit, showing ourselves to be His disciples (John 15:8).

John the Baptist warned the crowds that came to hear him preach, "The ax is already at the root of the trees, and every tree that does not produce good fruit will be cut down and thrown into the fire" (Luke 3:9). Such a tree is not necessarily rotten or stripped of its leaves, and from a distance may look like all the other trees. But walk by that tree at harvest time and it is soon obvious that the tree has a serious problem. It has no fruit! It has lost the ability to produce—the very reason for which it was created—and is only good to be cut up for firewood.

As you read this book, you may find areas in your Christian life where reevaluation and adjustment of priorities is needed because of the lack of spiritual fruit visible in your life. Don't be discouraged!

Each of us is unique. We each have a unique

personality, testimony, and social circle in which we move. Combined, these add up to the most telling fact of all—the many opportunities we each have to share the love of Christ with those around us. I hope that by the end of this book you will be better prepared to use these witnessing opportunities more effectively and become fruitful servants for our Lord Jesus Christ.

I pray that this book will become a learning tool which will help you cultivate a heart for others as you follow the witnessing style of Jesus.

Chapter One

Liberated to Witness

As Victor stood in front of the bathroom mirror, he marveled at his new life. His close friend Dan had led him to the Lord recently, and now Victor was preparing to go out and win other lost people to the Lord. He was excited by what lay ahead, and had jumped at the opportunity to join the church's evangelism team. At the orientation meeting the week before, the pastor had handed each person a witnessing script and instructed them to spend the following week memorizing it.

Dan told Victor that the Christian life would be a challenge, and Victor had found that to be true as he prepared for the team's first outreach. He knew that to be effective he'd have to overcome his shyness around strangers and somehow make his script sound like natural conversation. All of this had him standing in front of the bathroom mirror, practicing a natural presentation of his script.

He was halfway through his third attempt when his father yelled from the hall, "Victor, is that you?"

"Yes," Victor replied, frustrated that he had lost his place and would have to start over.

"What on earth are you doing? What's all this talking to yourself? Are you in love or something?"

Victor felt himself turning red. He wished he had practiced more quietly. How could he possibly make his atheistic father understand that he was preparing to share the greatest message in the world? "It's just some stuff for church. I'll be finished in a minute."

"Huh. Seems mighty odd to me," his father muttered as he shuffled down the hall. Victor waited a while before continuing his recitation more quietly.

Several minutes later, the bathroom door burst open. It was his sister Rachel.

"Victor, could you take me over to Janie's house? Mom said she would, but she had to work late. Dad said it's okay for you to use the car."

Victor could see the desperation in his sister's eyes. He knew Rachel was studying hard for an exam, and Janie was helping her. He glanced at his watch. "I'd really like to help you, but I don't have the time. I'm being picked up in five minutes to go witnessing."

Rachel looked like she would burst into tears, then she turned and ran out of the room.

Victor felt bad, but he didn't have time to dwell on it. He had to get his script delivery down pat.

A few minutes later a car horn sounded, and it wasn't long before Victor was swinging open the gate leading to his first witnessing stop of the evening. He knocked and eagerly waited for the door to open. His partner stood a step behind, praying.

The door jolted open. "What d'ya want?" grunted a dishevelled man clutching an amber bottle of beer. The man stared intently as Victor began his presentation. But somehow the man's stare dislodged both Victor's confidence and concentration. He began stumbling and stammering over the words he had memorized so meticulously. It had been easy in front of the mirror, but face to face with a real person was a different matter.

The man's glare turned to a sneer as Victor finally managed to blurt out a few stilted words about how he and his associate were from a local church and wanted to ask a few questions about religion.

"Well, I'm sorry. You came to the wrong house.

We don't go to church," the man gruffly replied as he swung the door shut in Victor's face.

Victor stood stunned for a moment. It hadn't gone at all like he'd expected. His partner quoted the words of Jesus to His disciples, "If anyone will not welcome you or listen to your words, shake the dust off your feet when you leave that home or town" (Matthew 10:14). Their confidence restored, they headed for the next house.

The little old lady at the house next door listened patiently and politely as Victor's partner gave his presentation. Then ever so sweetly, she cut in and told them that Mr. Grady down the street could certainly use their message.

Two hours later, after knocking on the door of every house on the street, Victor and his partner waited anxiously at the corner for the church van to pick them up. Victor gazed at the tally sheet in his hand. They had visited thirty homes. At eight of them there had been no answer. At nine the doors had been slammed in their faces, and at the other thirteen they had been cut short before they could finish their presentation. No one had shown any real interest in what they had to say.

Victor pondered how he could do a better job next time. He certainly needed to practice his delivery more. After all, he had been told what a great witnessing program it was. According to the pastor, thousands had been won to the Lord through it. Though discouraged, Victor committed himself to practice his witnessing script more before the evangelism team tried again the next week.

Witnessing as a Program

Victor's story illustrates a major obstacle we face in the Church today regarding witnessing. The problem is not that the majority of people are hard and unreceptive to the message of the Gospel. Rather, the problem is the "program mentality" that has grown up around witnessing. Witnessing has ceased to be something that flows naturally from our relationship with the Lord Jesus. Instead, it has become entrenched as a weekly church program where we learn certain techniques and go out to "do" them on others in the hope that they get "saved."[1]

Ministry from a biblical standpoint is not about *programs*, but about *people*. We are important to God. He made us to have fellowship with Him. He responds compassionately to us as individuals. He is intimately aware of our weaknesses and needs, and ministers to us accordingly. When He does, we feel special and loved by Him. But more often than not, program workers fail to see people as individuals. This seems particularly true of church witnessing programs. Rather than seeing non-Christians as unique individuals who are each special to God, they are too often viewed as potential members to fill the church pews and bolster the offering, or simply as impersonal "souls" to be saved.

As a pastor, I encourage congregations to engage in deliberate and strategically targeted witnessing efforts. However, we must be sure that these witnessing efforts do not take on a life of their own. We must not lose sight of the individual needs of the people we are commissioned to reach. Our emphasis should not be on programs, but where the Bible clearly places it—on people!

Throughout the Bible, God uses and anoints obedient men and women, not special programs. Methods and techniques are effective tools when placed in the hands of Spirit-led servants of God. They are not ends in themselves.

Front-door Evangelism

Another obstacle arises as we examine witnessing in the context of today's Church. Much of the evangelism energy of our churches is directed toward those men and women who walk through the front door of the church building. I like to call it "front-door evangelism."

Front-door evangelism emphasizes bringing people into the church rather than going out to meet them where they live. As a result, much effort is exerted trying to capture and hold on to church visitors through the use of door greeters, visitor cards and letters, altar calls, and special evangelistic meetings. The problem with this "come and see" attitude toward evangelism is that the average non-Christian will enter a church building usually only for a special event like a wedding or a funeral.[2]

Even if we successfully attract nonbelievers to the church, large group events like worship services and Sunday school classes are impersonal by their very nature. Large groups don't provide an atmosphere where intimate fellowship and care happen.

Although some front-door evangelism success can be realized, recent church growth research reveals that most non-Christians who enter the front doors of a church building rarely develop relationships with regular church members.[3] Since meaningful relationships do not develop quickly, most of these nonbelievers simply leave by the back door, never to return. This revolving-door syndrome plagues many local churches. As a pastor, I have personally experienced its frustrations.

Large group gatherings normally benefit the long-term church insiders, while the visitor or outsider is often left out, untouched by true, caring, biblical relationships.

Many of us believe that if we can just get a nonbeliever through the door of a church, we have done our job. We can then leave the person in the capable hands of someone more professional and proficient.

This tactic works better at getting a sick person through the doors of a hospital emergency room than in bringing nonbelievers into church. Once in the emergency room, we can fill out a registration card and leave the sick person in the care of trained nurses and doctors. We leave knowing we have faithfully done our part in delivering the sick person to those who have the training and experience to handle the situation.

However, when this strategy is used for evangelism, it is flawed and is doomed to failure. Christianity is not something to be administered to a person, as a doctor prescribes a drug or treatment. Church growth research reveals the grim reality that more than 70 percent of those individuals who make an initial response to Jesus Christ through the witness of a stranger never end up as growing and faithful members of a local church.[4] And the reality is that the pastor and most members of a congregation are strangers to nonbelievers the first time they visit a church.

Jesus never took anyone to a particular place to minister to them. He ministered to people where they were: in their homes, sitting by a well, on a mountainside, even on a boat in the middle of a raging storm.

We must be set free from the traditional program mentality and the isolationism of front-door evangelism. Witnessing is not something to be left to the professionals. Witnessing is far more than just getting a nonbeliever through the doors of a church. Witnessing is also much more than canned formulas and approaches that we try out on all those with whom we come into contact in the course of a day.

Victor's hypothetical story is experienced weekly by sincere Christians across our nation. However, if Christians took a few moments to analyze the way they came to the Lord, most would realize that it was mainly through a relative or friend, someone they knew and trusted. For Victor, it was through his friend Dan. And while Victor's zeal to share the Gospel with others was commendable, it was misguided. While he was out targeting strangers with whom he had no previous contact, he had left confusion at home. He had a very puzzled father who was probably wondering exactly what cult his son had managed to get himself into, and a sister who had received the message that a witnessing script was more important than her personal needs.

Many of us have allowed our spiritual priorities to become skewed. Like Martha in Luke 10:38-40, our efforts are often sincere, but misdirected. Instead, like Martha's sister Mary, we need to sit at the feet of Jesus, commune with Him, and absorb His heart for others.

The Gospel is the gift of God to us, and we are to pass it on to others. The saving power of the Gospel is not spread through impersonal presentations, but through transformed lives. As we spend time in the presence of the Lord, allowing Him to mold us into His image, our lives are transformed.

Becoming Ministers of the Gospel

When we think of the Church, we often think of either buildings or the institution of the church, with all its well-meaning liturgies and practices. But the truth of the matter is that you and I are the Church! When the New Testament speaks about the Church, it does not refer to physical structures or denominations. Instead, it talks about people—people who love and serve God.

When Paul referred to the Church in Ephesus, he did not mean a palatial building set on a hill. Rather, he was talking about all those in Ephesus who had accepted Jesus Christ as their Savior and Lord. They

were the Church in Ephesus! In the same way, we are
the Church.

Besides being the Church, we are also ministers
of the Gospel. I have a degree in theology and an
official position and title in a church, but that does
not make me any more a minister of the Gospel than
you, in the scriptural sense of the word. Any division
made within the Church in terms of our responsibility to minister to nonbelievers is artificial.

Peter tells us we are all "like living stones, [who]
are being built into a spiritual house to be a holy
priesthood, offering spiritual sacrifices acceptable to
God through Jesus Christ" (I Peter 2:5). Paul reminds
us that we are "co-heirs with Christ" (Romans 8:17).

Therefore, we must *all* minister the Gospel to
others. We cannot justify from Scripture an attitude
which would allow us to sit by and leave the sharing
of the Gospel to the Church's paid professionals.

The apostle Paul told the Ephesian Christians
that God had given to the Church certain gifted
individuals—apostles, prophets, evangelists, pastors, and teachers. However, he went on to explain
that God did not place them in the Church to do all
the work, but rather to train and equip the congregation to become active ministers of the Kingdom of
God (Ephesians 4:11-12). Everyone in the Church is
commissioned to minister the Gospel of Jesus Christ
in order to build up the Body of Christ and spread
the love of Jesus to those in our world who so badly
need His salvation.

Yet the sobering truth is that most of us are not
active ministers of the Gospel at all. We may occa-
sionally try to share the Gospel with another person,
but this is usually the exception rather than the rule.
I trust that by the time you finish reading this book,
you will be encouraged and challenged to minister
actively to those around you as a regular discipline

of your life, and, in so doing, do your part to fulfill Christ's Great Commission (see Matthew 28:16-20).

Becoming People-centered

Bill received a phone call from an old high school buddy he hadn't seen for several years. The friend asked Bill to join him for lunch, and Bill eagerly accepted the invitation. Bill looked forward with great anticipation to renewing his acquaintance with his old friend. But after arriving at the restaurant, Bill discovered that his buddy had only one thing in mind—to sell him some household products. Bill left deeply disappointed, feeling humiliated and discounted as a person. His friend didn't value him as a person, but only as a potential customer.

We are each capable of doing the same thing when we witness. However, nobody wins using this impersonal approach. The victims of impersonal witnessing are everywhere. They feel used, hurt, bitter, and dehumanized.

The Gospel is a life-changing message to be shared from a heart of compassion. When we adopt impersonal and domineering witnessing tactics, we end up reinforcing the stereotype that those who witness and share the Gospel publicly are either charlatans, oddballs, or misfits. I am constantly amazed by the number of Christians I meet who perceive witnessing as an anti-social, insensitive, unnatural, and overly aggressive activity. They believe this activity requires the violation of another person's privacy in socially unacceptable ways in order to share the Gospel with them.

It is time to turn this around. It is time for Christians to be liberated from impersonal methods! Christianity is first and foremost a relationship with Jesus Christ. The best, most fruitful way for you to draw others into a relationship with Him is through a relationship with you! Yes, *you!* You have spiritual gifts and abilities and social contacts that other Christians do not have. You have unique opportunities and divine appointments to share the Gospel. As you will discover in the following chapters, there *is* an effective way to witness which doesn't require you to embrace unnatural methods and impersonal scripts. It only requires that you fall in love with Jesus and be willing to be molded into His image.

Chapter Two

Treasure in Jars of Clay

"But we have this treasure in jars of clay to show that this all-surpassing power is from God and not from us" (II Corinthians 4:7). God has filled our lives with His treasure. God has put His presence within us as a testimony to others of His all-surpassing power and love.

It is tragic that many of us are more concerned about the clay jar than we are about God's treasure inside. Somehow we think our clay jar has too many imperfections or is not as good as another person's. We believe that our human weaknesses somehow negate the value of God's presence dwelling inside.

Let's put it another way. We have been touched by the power of the Gospel and have the living God dwelling within. Yet we still think we lack the ability to be an effective witness because we are not gifted in evangelism, don't have a stunning testimony, or don't know the Bible well enough.

This misconception belittles the power and grace of God in our lives. We *can* be effective witnesses for the Lord Jesus Christ! God doesn't look for specially gifted people, but for willing hearts that He can use.

Why I Can't Witness

Following are five common misconceptions about witnessing. Read through these prayerfully, and ask yourself whether you have subconsciously accepted any or all of these misconceptions. Each one can have a paralyzing effect on our ability to witness effectively. If we properly deal with these misconceptions in our lives, we have begun the transforming process of becoming the kind of witness God wants us to be.

"I am not a gifted evangelist."

It is true that there is such a thing as a gifted evangelist. Paul lists the evangelist as one of God's gifts to the Church (Ephesians 4:11). Church growth studies indicate that in the average local church, about ten percent of a congregation will be gifted by God as evangelists.[5]

But God has given a diversity of gifts to His people, and all of them are vitally important in fulfilling the Church's witnessing commission to the world. Regardless of what spiritual gift God has given to us as our contribution to the Body of Christ, each of us is still commanded to be a witness for Him. "You will receive power when the Holy Spirit comes on you; and you will be my witnesses in Jerusalem, and in all Judea and Samaria, and to the ends of the earth" (Acts 1:8). While ten percent may be gifted as evangelists, each of us is clearly responsible to be Christ's witness.

To understand this responsibility, compare it to teaching. While some of us may be gifted to stand before a congregation and teach the Word of God, each parent has the duty to teach the ways of God to his children. We do not have the option of saying, "I'm not very good at teaching, so I won't try it."

While you may not be a Billy Graham, you have a unique position to fill. The first step toward true revival and dynamic church growth is for each of us to embrace the spiritual task God has given him to do, and to serve Him with all his heart, soul, and mind (Matthew 22:37).

"I am not good enough to be a witness for God."

This is a concern which many of us have. No

sooner do we begin to tell another person about Christ than we remember all the times we have failed. Before we fall into condemnation, we should ponder the following points:

Satan is the one who accuses us before God (Revelation 12:10), but Jesus Christ is even now interceding for us (Hebrews 7:25). Satan would like nothing better than to defeat us before we begin, leaving us joyless and condemned. But Jesus is cheering us on, praying for us as we fall short, and lifting us up to begin again. If we always feel that we're not morally fit to witness, we have fallen prey to the lies of Satan.

All of us need the grace of God in our lives. "If we claim to be without sin, we deceive ourselves and the truth is not in us. If we confess our sins, he is faithful and just and will forgive us our sins and purify us from all unrighteousness" (I John 1:8-9). These verses are explicit. None of us is "good enough." We have all sinned; we have all failed to meet God's standards at various points in our lives (Romans 3:23). The important issue is not that we fail to meet God's standard from time to time, but rather how we respond when we do.

Too many of us take the route that leads to condemnation, where we are tossed about on a stormy sea of Satan's lies. But it doesn't have to be so. First John 1:8-9 holds a promise. The bad news is that we have all sinned, but the good news—the promise—is that God will forgive us and restore us if we honestly confess our sins to Him and ask for His forgiveness. There is no biblical reason for us to ever again think we are not morally good enough to be a witness for Jesus Christ.

We are witnessing to the truth. After Jesus delivered the demonized man in the region of the Gerasenes, the man begged to go with Jesus and the disciples. But Jesus refused and told him instead,

"Return home and tell how much God has done for you" (Luke 8:39). Was that man morally perfect? No. Did he need to be? No. All Jesus asked him to do was to go and tell everyone what Jesus had done for him. To be faithful to Jesus' witnessing commission, we simply need to experience the touch of Jesus in our lives and be excited enough about it to share with others what He has done for us.

When Peter addressed the crowds at Solomon's Colonnade, he emphasized God's ability, not his own: "Men of Israel,...why do you stare at us as if by our own power or godliness we had made this man walk?...By faith in the name of Jesus, this man whom you see and know was made strong. It is Jesus' name and the faith that comes through him that has given this complete healing to him..." (Acts 3:12,16).

The world is not looking for perfect Christians, but rather for honest Christians. They are looking for those of us who are willing to admit to ourselves and to others that we are not only sinners *saved* by God's grace, but that we are also sinners *kept* by His grace. Such honesty is a powerful witness to the crooked and perverse world in which we live.

"I don't know my Bible well enough."

Certainly it is true that the better we know our Bible, the more proficient we will be in answering difficult questions. However, this in no way implies that you must be a Bible scholar before you can be a witness for the Lord Jesus. All it means is that if you are a Bible scholar, you can more accurately answer the questions non-Christians might ask about God and the Bible.

God does not want us to be ignorant about His word. Yet at the same time, we do not need a Bible college degree to share the basic message of the Gospel with those we meet. Witnessing is telling others what God has done for us, not debating the answers to difficult questions. Yes, there are difficult questions which deserve well-researched answers, and we should equip ourselves as best as we can. But not knowing all the answers does not negate our ability or responsibility to witness.

Have you ever wondered how the early Church witnessed? Along with the use of the Old Testament, they often used testimonies of how God had touched their lives as the basis for their witnessing. "You yourselves are our letter, written on our hearts, known and read by everybody" (II Corinthians 3:2).

We are still to be God's living letters in the world—a testimony of His love for mankind. Don't be misguided: being His living witnesses does not mean we must all be Bible scholars.

"I'm not an extrovert."

Many of us believe that we cannot be effective witnesses for Christ because we don't have outgoing personalities. Unfortunately, we forget that it is God who created us and endowed us with our unique personalities.

God did not mean for our personalities to be hindrances or excuses for inactivity. Rather, He gave us our personalities so we could be His unique witnesses in the world. No one else is like you; no two people are exactly the same. God purposed it that way so that through all His people He could reveal to a needy world a multi-faceted picture of who He is.

Each of us is a special instrument in God's hands. So relax; be yourself. God will use you regardless of whether you're an introvert or an extrovert.

"I don't have an exciting testimony."

As a pastor, I have the privilege of interviewing Christians who desire to become members of our church. In the process I listen to their personal testimonies, and I am continually amazed at the different means God uses to draw people into His Kingdom. Each testimony is unique, giving glory to the grace and love of God in a special way. Yet when those same people are challenged with opportunities to witness, many reply that their testimony is dull and boring. How can this be? What's boring and "ho-hum" about having the risen Christ dwell within you and being transformed from death to life?

It is unfortunate that so much attention is focused on spectacular testimonies. It's true that many people need to hear of a way out of their bondage, be it the misuse of sex, physical abuse, or substance abuse. Yet there are just as many people who need to know that God also offers help and hope to those enmeshed in the normal routine of life.

Take a frazzled housewife with three children under four years of age. She may well be impressed by a spectacular testimony she sees on television or reads about in a magazine. But she is far more likely to be touched when the woman next door volunteers to care for her children, then shares how God gave her a new sense of self-worth and peace in a trying situation.

Every testimony has a place, and yours fits somewhere. Each of us is a product of God's grace, regardless how mundane we may think our testimony is. Your testimony is well worth sharing.

Credentials of the Heart

There is more to being a witness than just confronting our fears and dealing with excuses. There are also a number of credentials that God looks for in our lives. I like to call them *credentials of the heart*. These are certain dispositions which will allow God to work effectively through us as His witnesses.

God is not so interested in the excuses listed in the previous section. Those are obstacles that we must overcome. But God is particularly concerned with our heart motivations. God does not offer us a witnessing plan. We *are* His witnesses! And as His witnesses, our character speaks the loudest for Him. That is why God looks for Christians of strong character, whose hearts are willing, open, and pliable.

As you read through these heart credentials, prayerfully allow the Holy Spirit to penetrate those areas of your life which need His touch.

A Growing Heart-to-Heart Relationship with God

Anyone desiring to be a witness for Christ must first experience His love and grace in his own life. We cannot give away what we do not have. We cannot introduce someone to a person we do not personally know. Neither can we trumpet forth the Gospel message with conviction unless we have first proved its validity in our own lives.

Jesus told the Pharisees that "out of the overflow of the heart the mouth speaks" (Matthew 12:34). If our hearts are not filled with love for God, it will soon be shown by our words and actions. We cannot expect to draw a person any closer to Jesus than we are ourselves, nor can we be demonstrations of God's truths unless we live by them. Words without action, or truth without demonstration, is hypocrisy.

Sadly, many of us attempt to witness for Jesus from a feeling of religious duty rather than out of the overflow of a daily personal relationship with Him. But try as we may, living water will simply not flow from a dry well.

Before setting out as a witness for our Lord Jesus, our first concern must be our vibrant and growing daily relationship with Him. Only then will we become the effective witnesses He longs for us to be.

A Pliable and Teachable Heart

"You are the Potter, I am the clay....Mold me and make me after Your will, while I am waiting, yielded and still." The words of this chorus are based on

Jeremiah 18, and serve as a good reminder of the role God wants to play in our Christian lives. We are to be like pliable clay in the skilled hands of an expert potter.

True disciples humble themselves under God's authority and ask Him to shape them into men and women of God. They don't shrink from God's hand of correction and leading in their lives. They know "the Lord disciplines those he loves" (Hebrews 12:6).

An Honest Heart

We are often afraid to admit our humanity with all its weaknesses. As a result, we attempt to live behind a false mask of self-assurance. The sad fact is that everyone knows it is not real. Being a witness for Christ is not pretending to be something or someone we are not. Rather, it is allowing God to shine through who we really are—human beings.

In His eternal wisdom and by His sovereign choice, God has determined to communicate His redemptive purposes through human beings. More than anyone else, He knows we are not perfect, yet He chose to use us. The least we can do is be honest with Him and with each other about the frailty of our humanness.

And because we are human, we feel what other people feel. We understand how they hurt when faced with the loss of a loved one, when they have been laid off work, or when they have been overtaken by depression and despair. Our honesty about how we have experienced these feelings and how Christ has helped us deal with them is a powerful point of witness.

God cannot use phonies and fakes; He can only use those of us who are honest—honest with Him and honest with each other. We don't have to be "saints," or project some religious pose to the world to be effective witnesses. We simply have to be honest and transparent.

A Willing Heart

Jesus did what the Father told Him to—nothing more and nothing less. Jesus said in John 6:38, "For I have come down from heaven not to do my will but to do the will of him who sent me." God uses those who are ready and willing to witness for Him to anyone, anytime, anywhere, and under any circumstances.

It is said that God values availability over ability. Many of us question why we don't sense the specific leading of the Holy Spirit in witnessing on a daily basis. But even if God specifically led us to witness to a non-Christian, we would not always be obedient. God will only lead those Christians He knows will obey Him. He is looking for those who are available to do what He asks, not necessarily for those who possess extraordinary abilities.

A Fully Prepared Heart

Paul makes it clear that our witness as Christians is not always easy. "For our struggle is not against flesh and blood, but against the rulers, against the authorities, against the powers of this dark world and against the spiritual forces of evil in heavenly realms" (Ephesians 6:12). We are engaged in a battle for the hearts and minds of men and women. It is not a physical battle, but rather a spiritual battle.

The recent war in the Persian Gulf provides a vivid illustration for us. The countries allied under the auspices of the United Nations poured their best trained fighting forces into Saudi Arabia. On the other side, large numbers of war-seasoned Iraqi foot soldiers were amassed along the borders of Kuwait and Iraq. The Allies' greatest fear was that, when the battle began, the experienced Iraqi troops would overwhelm the Allied forces.

The ground battle did begin, and ended only hours later, with Allied troops victorious and the Iraqi soldiers beaten and dejected. The Allied soldiers were simply better prepared than the Iraqis, many of whom were young, poorly trained, ill-equipped draftees. If you want to win a war, you must be committed to send your best soldiers into the battle!

It is the same in the Kingdom of God. God is looking for Christians who are fully prepared to engage in the battle that rages for the hearts and souls of men. He is looking for those of us dressed in our spiritual armor and ready for the battle (Ephesians 6:14-18).[6] To become an effective witness for Christ means having our hearts fully prepared so God can use us.

As we conclude this chapter, I trust you have prayerfully examined the common misconceptions which keep many of us from being effective witnesses for Jesus Christ. I also trust you have become familiar with the credentials of the heart, for without them, our witnessing efforts will be short-lived and incomplete.

For many of us, what we say and how we live are two different things. Too often, we perceive that God's message is separate from us as messengers. As we shall see in the next chapter, this is a false perception. For we are not only the messengers, but also the message!

Chapter Three

Message or Messenger

Let's return to Victor, the young man we met in Chapter One. Victor had a breakdown in communication. He was talking, but people weren't listening. His words carried the outline of God's plan for salvation, but didn't penetrate the hearts and minds of the people to whom he was speaking. As a result, Victor was not communicating. His words may have been meaningful, but unless they were received and understood by the other person, they were wasted.

I'm sure all of us have experienced situations when we have been talking to another person but did not communicate with them. Why is this? How is it possible to speak to a person and yet not communicate with them?

The answer is not complicated. Studies have shown that for effective spoken communication to occur, three essential ingredients must be present: the actual words we say, our tone of voice (attitude), and nonverbal mannerisms. What is important is the percentage each ingredient plays in producing effective communication.

Ninety-three percent of effective communication is tone of voice and nonverbal mannerisms, and only seven percent is actually dependent upon the words we verbalize.[7] Or put another way, the attitude and manner in which we say something actually communicates more to a person than the words we say. So it's possible to speak to someone and not really communicate with them. While we might be saying the right words, our attitude and manner may be communicating a different message—a negative nonverbal message—so people stop listening to our words.

Victor's message was memorized and artificial. He wasn't really sensitive to the people he met. What was important to Victor was delivering his scripted Gospel presentation.

Those of us who constantly experience communication breakdown when we attempt to witness to non-Christians are too often approaching witnessing solely as a verbal activity. Rebecca Manley Pippert makes the following pertinent observation in her book, *Out of the Saltshaker:* "The way we communicate is as important as what we communicate. In fact the two cannot really be separated. Our attitude and style communicate content just as do our words. If we notice that non-Christians seem embarrassed, apologetic and defensive, it is probably because they are picking up *our* attitude."[8]

What does all this mean, and what are the ramifications for Christians? Clearly the message of the Gospel is linked closely to the character of the person communicating it. We are both the *messenger* and the *message*! God has commissioned us to go forth with the Gospel as His messengers, but at the same time we are to embody that message. We are to live it out for all to see. We are to demonstrate to people that the message of the Gospel does not exist only in words. It is not some abstract idea, but rather God's good news to man, which is validated through our daily lives as Christians.

This is exactly what Jesus did. During His earthly life He demonstrated that God's Word was true and that we could live as He did. For "whoever claims to live in him must walk as Jesus did" (I John 2:6).

Jesus—The Icon of God

Colossians 1:15 tells us that Jesus was the exact

image of God. The Greek word translated "image" is *icon*. Jesus was God's icon. He reflected what God was really like. "Anyone who has seen me has seen the Father," He told the disciples in John 14:9. Jesus was the exact image of God's character in all its perfection and glory. He did not simply *declare* truth; through His life He *demonstrated* truth.

The apostle Paul reminds us in I Corinthians 4:20, "For the kingdom of God is not a matter of talk but of power." Jesus didn't come just to talk, but to be a powerful representation of who God was. He preached to multitudes and taught individuals in their homes, by the Sea of Galilee, and along the way. But every time He spoke, His inspiring words were supported by the power of the life He lived. His life validated the message He came to reveal. He was not just another prophet sent by God; He was truth incarnate—He was "God with us" (Matthew 1:23; John 1:1,14).

Jesus came in stark contrast to the religious leaders of His day, the Pharisees. The Pharisees were masters of many words. They knew the talk. They could argue theology all day long. They also kept an elaborate system of rules they had constructed for themselves.

Yet, despite their religious talk and outward piety, the Pharisees were internally empty and void of God's character. They were hypocrites, and Jesus addressed them as such on several occasions. "Woe to you, teachers of the law and Pharisees, you hypocrites! You shut the kingdom of heaven in men's faces..." (Matthew 23:13).[9]

Jesus was the opposite of the religious leaders. He came to embody God's law, to demonstrate how people could live a holy life free from the hypocrisy of the religious establishment of His day. And throngs of people were attracted to Him. The Gos-

pels record that multitudes of people followed Jesus,
yet didn't always understand what Jesus meant. But
they continued to follow Him. Why? Because His
words were matched by a lifestyle that was genuine
and transparent.

The New Testament condemns the separation of
our words and our lifestyle. "What good is it, my
brothers, if a man claims to have faith but has no
deeds? Can such faith save him? Suppose a brother
or sister is without clothes and daily food. If one of
you says to him, 'Go, I wish you well; keep warm
and well fed,' but does nothing about his physical
needs, what good is it? In the same way, faith by
itself, if it is not accompanied by action, is dead"
(James 2:14-17). James is explicit here. Faith must
flow into practice; words must flow into action. The
truth of God in our hearts must produce a changed
life that accurately reflects God's character.

Because of this truth, the religious leaders came
under the judgment of Jesus even more than prostitutes and tax collectors who openly confessed their
lack of righteousness. The Pharisees lacked integrity.
They were unwilling to recognize or acknowledge
that their lives did not match their words. As Jesus
warned us, "...unless your righteousness surpasses
that of the Pharisees and the teachers of the law, you
will certainly not enter the kingdom of heaven"
(Matthew 5:20).

The person who is able to verbalize a Gospel
outline in three minutes is not always the most effective witness; it's the one who consistently models the
lifestyle of Jesus. As someone once said to me, "The
best argument for the Christian faith is Christians—
their joy, love, and wholeness."

Modeling Jesus

We have a tendency in the Church to isolate specific incidents in the life of Jesus and construct elab-

orate doctrines around them. This is especially true when we talk about Jesus and witnessing. We tend to take a situation such as Jesus' encounter with the Samaritan woman at the well and lift from it what we see as the essence of Jesus' witnessing style. This reduces Jesus' witnessing approach to a formula.

As I have said, there are weaknesses and dangers when we reduce witnessing to a formula that we can apply in every situation. The most cursory reading of the Gospels will show that Jesus didn't use a formula. His approach to the Samaritan woman at the well was not the same as His approach when speaking with the woman caught in adultery (John 4:1-42; 8:3-11).

Rather than trying to isolate some witnessing formula Jesus may have used, we need to observe His entire life and see how it affected the people He met. The Gospels contain eyewitness accounts of the life of Jesus (Luke 1:2-3; John 20:30; 21:24; I John 1:1). They were written so we could see Jesus' overall way of living. As we survey the Gospels, what do we find? How did Jesus relate to people?

A Heart for Others

Jesus was not a "holier than thou" separatist Instead, He lived and ministered among common people, touching their lives with God's love. As a result, He was loved and accepted by the average folk, but rejected by the religious establishment.

The religious leaders criticized Jesus because He ministered in Galilee and not in Jerusalem, He didn't keep the Sabbath properly, He physically touched lepers to heal them, and He talked with and forgave prostitutes. Jesus was a friend of sinners. He actively sought them out and declared that He had "not come to call the righteous, but sinners" (Matthew 9:13).

Jesus not only befriended sinners, but He refused to let religious, social, or ethnic barriers stand in His way. For example, the Samaritans were despised by the Jews because of their religious beliefs, but Jesus ministered to a Samaritan woman at Jacob's well (John 4:1-42). He also healed the son of a Roman official (John 4:43-53), touched and healed social outcasts like lepers (Luke 5:12-16), and called a tax collector to be His disciple (Matthew 9:9).

Jesus had compassion for people. He was neither indifferent to their pain and suffering nor merely intellectually concerned. Instead, He emotionally bonded with suffering people and reached out to them. He anguished over their helpless condition. When Jesus received the news of Lazarus' death, He wept (John 11:35). When Jesus looked at the crowds of people who came to hear Him, He "had compassion on them, because they were harassed and helpless, like sheep without a shepherd" (Matthew 9:36).

Jesus was approachable, and He loved people. He spent time with them, ate with them, visited their homes, and attended their parties and weddings. He enjoyed being with people, and they enjoyed being with Him. He treated them with love and respect as God's special creations. He affirmed their value.

People knew Jesus cared about them. The way He lived His life portrayed that fact. So they flocked to Him, sat with Him, talked with Him, and listened to Him as He taught them about the Kingdom of God.

Jesus knew that for the Gospel to be good news, it needed to be delivered with great love and sensitivity. So that was how He approached people. There was no "one size fits all" formula. To Him each person was a uniquely created individual. He listened as they spoke, and adapted the message of the Kingdom of God to meet their personal needs.

It is a sad commentary on the state of Christianity today that all too often we fail to demonstrate a deep-rooted love for other people. However, if we desire to become effective witnesses for Christ, we must first become people-centered. We must become a friend of sinners, as Jesus was.

For some, this may seem frightening at first, but it shouldn't be. Our fears are often derived from an unscriptural value judgment. Some of us mistakenly believe that we are intrinsically better than non-Christians, and that if we spend time around sinners, their sinful lifestyle will somehow rub off on us.

However, this is not God's perspective. All human beings are valuable to Him, and He loves each one. His unconditional love for us is not based on anything we can do to earn it, but because He created us. That is the message Jesus embodied—that God loves and esteems His creatures. And that is the message we must live out as His followers.

A Man of Prayer

Not only did Jesus have a heart for others, but He was also a man of prayer. The one directly follows the other. Prayer was not an optional extra that Jesus squeezed in when He had the time—it was imperative! He rose early in the morning and escaped to a quiet place where He could be alone and pray (Mark 1:35). "It [prayer] was more than an occasional practice on his part; it was a lifelong habit. It was an attitude of mind and heart—an atmosphere in which he lived; the very air he breathed. Everything he did arose out of prayer."[10]

Jesus recognized that His spiritual strength came through spending intimate time with His Father. Many of us mistakenly believe that Jesus was able to do all He did on earth because He was God. It is true that He was God. But in becoming a human being, He made Himself "nothing, taking the very nature of a servant" (Philippians 2:7). In other words, He gave up His right to act as God and walked as a servant, in perfect obedience to the Father. "'My food,' said Jesus, 'is to do the will of him who sent me and to finish his work'" (John 4:34). Through prayer Jesus learned to rely upon the leading and empowerment of the Holy Spirit.[11]

Prayer was the logical conclusion to Jesus' heart concern for people. It was an act of ultimate compassion as He interceded before His Father on behalf of the people with whom He had personal contact.

Often we fail to see prayer in this light. Prayer becomes something we squeeze into our schedule because the Bible admonishes Christians to pray. When the going gets tough, prayer is often the first thing we drop from our daily activities. But prayer and intercession for others is born out of a compassionate heart. When we are filled with God's love, we are willing to sacrifice our time in order to lift up people and their needs before the Lord, entreating Him to move on their behalf.

The more we pray, the more our compassion for people grows. The more our compassion grows, the more we desire to intercede for others. So it is no wonder that Jesus, who was love incarnate, prayed to His Father about everything.

Becoming the Message

Several years ago, I had the opportunity to study in Israel. I traveled extensively throughout the country, and especially enjoyed the area around the Sea of Galilee. During my frequent visits to this region, I fell in love with the historical life and ministry of Jesus. While there, I read and reread the Gospels, imagining what it must have been like to follow Jesus. I imagined the beaming faces of the people as they watched Jesus perform miracles. I also tried to picture in my mind their bewilderment as He spoke to them in parables about the Kingdom of God.

Even today, I can close my eyes and recall that corner of the world and what it must have been like in Jesus' day. I have meditated and pondered much on the ministry of Jesus over the years. While the penetrating words of Jesus were extremely important, people were especially attracted to His character, which was exemplified in the life He lived. He came not only to declare God's message of love, but also to demonstrate through His life how that message could change lives. He wasn't just a messenger; He was the message incarnate.

If we are to be successful witnesses for the Lord Jesus Christ, we must follow Jesus' example. We must *become* the message. We must live and reflect the message of the Gospel in every area of our lives. As the apostle Paul emphasizes, "You show that you are a letter from Christ, the result of our ministry, written not with ink but with the Spirit of the living God, not on tablets of stone but on tablets of human hearts" (II Corinthians 3:3). A paraphrase of this verse could read, "You are a letter from Christ for all to read. You're not a letter to be read like ink on paper, or listened to like words from a dissertation, but a letter carried on the actions that flow from your heart."

Are we Christ's letter to the world? Are we a living embodiment of the message of the Gospel? Do we reflect and project Christ's love to everyone with whom we come in contact? Or are we more concerned about delivering our memorized, prepackaged Gospel presentation? Are we simply the messenger, or are we also the message for others to see and follow?

Chapter Four

Disciples, Not Decisions

"10,000 Saved in the Philippines!" announced the bold, black headline across the top of the missionary newsletter. I read the letter with great interest. It indicated that 10,000 people had been led in repeating the sinner's prayer at the end of a series of mass evangelistic rallies. Such response is certainly admirable. However, the article seemed to communicate that these 10,000 were now disciples of Jesus Christ.

In my understanding, the writer of the article had confused *decisions* with *disciples*, a tragic mistake that many of us make. It is no wonder that we have spiritually immature Christians and a high attrition rate among those who make momentary decisions for Jesus Christ.

Most of us are familiar with the Great Commission that Jesus gave to His disciples before His ascension into heaven. When we read it, do we understand what the words really mean, or what someone has told us they mean? "All authority in heaven and on earth has been given to me. Therefore go and *make disciples* of all nations, *baptizing* them in the name of the Father and of the Son and of the Holy Spirit, and *teaching* them to obey everything I have commanded you. And surely I will be with you always, to the very end of the age" (Matthew 28:18-20, italics mine).

The first thing we notice is that Jesus commands us to make disciples, not simply to solicit decisions. In making a person a disciple, we are to baptize them and teach them. Baptism signifies the public confession of a person's new birth in Christ. And just like parents who teach their children over time to become adults, we also are to teach newborn Christians how to become mature people in the Lord.

As Great Commission Christians, our goal should be to make *more* and *better* disciples. This goal is not achieved by someone reciting a sinner's prayer. Disciple-making takes time and energy on the part of the person doing the teaching and the person who is the learner.

Yes, it's important that every non-Christian make a willful and personal commitment to receive Jesus as Lord and Savior (Romans 10:9). But this is only the first step in becoming a mature disciple. We are not only called to offer free passage to heaven after death; we are also called to teach people how to live daily for the Lord Jesus Christ now!

Church growth expert Peter Wagner defines evangelism like this: "To evangelize is so to present Christ Jesus in the power of the Holy Spirit, that men and women will come to put their trust in God through Him, to accept Him as their Saviour, and serve Him as their King in the fellowship of His Church."[12]

If we accept this definition, a person would not be numbered a true disciple of Jesus Christ until he has personally received Him as his Savior and King, *and* has become an active, growing member of a local church fellowship.

It follows, then, that the act of reciting the sinner's prayer and inviting Christ into our life is just one step on the way to becoming a mature disciple. Conversion is a process, not simply a momentary decision. It is also helpful to note that the conversion process doesn't begin at the moment of decision, but much further back.

Although not precise, the following diagram (known as the Engel Scale) is a helpful tool in visualizing this process.[13] It records the various steps a person often goes through on the way to becoming a faithful, growing disciple of Christ. Study the diagram from the bottom up.

+3 *A lifetime of conceptual and behavioral growth in Christ*
+2 *Incorporation into a local Body of Christ*
+1 *Post-decision evaluation*
  0 *The person is born again, and becomes a new creation in Christ.*
-1 *Repentance and faith in Christ*
-2 *Decision to act*
-3 *Personal problem recognition*
-4 *Positive attitude toward the Gospel*
-5 *Grasp of the implications of the Gospel*
-6 *Awareness of the fundamentals of the Gospel*
-7 *Initial awareness of the Gospel*
-8 *Awareness of a supreme being, but no effective knowledge of the Gospel*

This diagram moves from the bottom, "Awareness of a supreme being, but no effective knowledge of the Gospel," to the top, "A lifetime of conceptual and behavioral growth in Christ." To get from the bottom to the top, a person normally moves through each of the stages in the conversion process, though not uniformly. Some people move very rapidly through these stages; others don't. Still others may come only so far in the process and stall.

It is important in sharing the Gospel with a person that we accurately assess where he is presently located on the Engel Scale. Such an assessment will help us discern more effectively how we share the Gospel with him. For example, perhaps he was raised in a Christian home. We could assume then that he falls on the scale at about level -5, since he is likely to have a reasonable "grasp of the implications of the Gospel." That is probably the level where we need to start in sharing the Gospel with him. It is unlikely that we need to spend time convincing him of the existence of a supreme being.

Another important thing to remember is that the conversion process takes time to accomplish. It is highly unlikely that we are going to influence a person to move from level -8 to +3 by sharing the Gospel with him once. What we should aim for in our witnessing is to move the person up a step or two in the conversion process. However, even this may take days, months, or possibly years to accomplish.

One other way to understand the conversion process is to compare it to the three stages in the birth of a child: the nine months of pre-birth formation in the mother's womb, the actual birth event, and the integration of the new baby into the family.

In comparison, the spiritual conversion process also involves three stages: the pre-evangelism formation prior to conversion, the born-again event, and the integration of the new Christian into the family of God (a local church fellowship), where he can be nurtured as he grows spiritually.

The following diagram compares the Engel Scale to the three spiritual conversion stages.

Conversion Stages

-8	-7	-6	-5	-4	-3	-2	-1	0	+1	+2	+3
Pre-evangelism Formation						Born-again Event			Assimilation Discipleship		

We need to see ourselves as part of a team God uses in guiding a person through the stages of conversion. He doesn't expect us to do it all! Thus we should not consider ourselves failures at witnessing when a person does not accept Christ the first time we share the Gospel. Neither should we take all the credit when a person does accept Christ. We were merely the person at the end of the process; God allowed us to experience the joy of harvesting.

It's much like a football game. A wide receiver may actually carry the ball over the goal line for a touchdown, but it has been the combined and coordinated effort of the whole team that brought it about. God sovereignly coordinates the efforts of a team of Christians in moving a person through the conversion process. The glory in any conversion, however, ultimately belongs to God alone!

People in Process

I have created the following Resistance/Receptivity diagram, which includes three categories of people—left, middle, and right—whom we will all encounter in the process of sharing the Gospel.[14]

People Categories

Left-end People		Middle People		Right-end People	
Hostile	Resistant	Indifferent	Interested	Receptive	Producers

This diagram clearly illustrates that we must use the proper approach to help non-Christians move from left to right, from enemies of the Gospel to producers in God's Kingdom. Let's take a closer look at these three categories of people.

Left-end People

This category includes those who are hostile, even dangerous, to those who are merely resistant to the Gospel. The soil of their hearts is packed down as hard as cement, and the seed of God's Word cannot penetrate the surface to germinate, take root, and grow. When left-end people hear the Gospel message, they deliberately reject it. Indeed, many left-end people often respond to the Gospel message and messenger with visible resistance, ranging from simple ridicule to persecution and even physical harm.

When witnessing to those at this extreme, we must remember that our battle isn't against flesh and blood. Non-Christians aren't our enemies. John White puts it this way: "A favorable reaction does not mean you are witnessing skillfully any more than a hostile reaction means that you have blown it. By all means be self-critical and check to see whether you have not been tactless, rude, critical, discourteous or opinionated. However, the reaction may tell you something not about yourself but about the person to whom you are bearing witness."[15]

Saul, later to become Paul, was a clear example of a left-end person. Acts 7:54-60 tells how he consented to Stephen's death by stoning. Saul was a man who was definitely both hostile and vocal about his rejection of the Gospel. Bar-Jesus is another example. Luke described him as a Jewish false prophet who set about to hinder the Roman proconsul from accepting Paul's message (Acts 13:8).

In the Gospels, Jesus classified entire villages as left-end people. "And you, Capernaum, will you be lifted up to the skies? No, you will go down to the depths. If the miracles that were performed in you had been performed in Sodom, it would have remained to this day. But I tell you that it will be more bearable for Sodom on the day of judgment than for you" (Matthew 11:23-24).

Despite the fact that left-end people are resistant to the Gospel, we must have a heart of compassion for them. They are objects of God's love, and His greatest gift of love to them is the Gospel message.

Middle People

This group includes those who are indifferent to the Gospel, as well as those who are interested. The indifferent do not reveal any sense of personal conviction or concern about the truth of God. The interested, on the other hand, are those non-Christians who are honest seekers of truth.

Middle people are not quite ready to make an informed decision to follow Jesus as Savior and Lord. However, they're usually open to receive more information and exposure to the Christian faith.

Again, there are many examples of these people in Scripture. The rich young ruler is an obvious choice. He came to Jesus sincerely wanting to know more about gaining eternal life. He wanted to know the choices he had to weigh (Matthew 19:16-30).

Sergius Paulus, the Roman proconsul, is another good example (Acts 13:7), as is King Agrippa (Acts 25:23 to 26:32).

Right-end People

This category includes those who are receptive to the Gospel, plus those who are productive members of God's Kingdom. Through the Holy Spirit they have made an informed choice to receive Christ. They are ready to make Christ their Lord and Savior.

The Bereans are an example of a group of people who could be classified as right-end people. "Now the Bereans were of more noble character than the Thessalonians, for they received the message with great eagerness and examined the Scriptures every day to see if what Paul said was true" (Acts 17:11).

Producers, on the other hand, are those people who have grown beyond the initial born-again decision to become mature Christians. Biblical examples of right-end people are Cornelius (Acts 10), the Ethiopian eunuch (Acts 8:26-39), Lydia (Acts 16:11-15), and Crispus (Acts 18:7-8).

Tending the Garden

In I Corinthians 3:6-7 Paul writes, "I planted the seed, Apollos watered it, but God made it grow. So neither he who plants nor he who waters is anything, but only God, who makes things grow." Paul compares evangelism activities to farming. The soil must be cultivated, the seed planted and watered, and the field tended until a crop is mature and harvested. All the while, Paul makes it clear that it is God who does the real work. He is the one who causes the seed to germinate, take root, and grow.

Using a farming analogy, I have identified five areas of evangelism—cultivating, sowing, watering, harvesting, and storing. Each of these areas summarizes a certain aspect of our witnessing efforts, and all are closely linked to the process of conversion (see following diagram).

Evangelism Activities

1	2	3	4	5
Cultivating	Sowing	Watering	Harvesting	Storing

Cultivating the Soil

The first step in farming is to cultivate or prepare the soil for planting. This often involves plowing up the hard compact soil and removing any obstacles that would impede the growth of the seed. Spiritually speaking, cultivating the soil includes preparing the heart of a non-Christian through caring friendship, good works, spiritual warfare, and intercessory prayer, so that they will eventually be open and receptive to the Gospel message.

Cultivating is also called pre-evangelism, and is based upon the premise that demonstration of the Gospel precedes persuasion. Cultivation is often the hardest work in evangelism. Jesus said, "I sent you to reap what you have not worked for. Others have done the *hard work,* and you have reaped the benefits of their labor" (John 4:38, italics mine).

Sowing the Seed

After cultivating the soil comes sowing the seed. Sowing in evangelism is where we directly share the Gospel message with a non-Christian whose heart is softened and open. Following are some practical tips to use when engaged in sowing this message.

Sow on cultivated soil. Jesus instructs us not to sow seed on unprepared soil. "Do not give dogs what is sacred; do not throw your pearls to pigs. If you do, they may trample them under their feet, and then turn and tear you to pieces" (Matthew 7:6).

Many of us want to skip the hard work of cultivating, so we attempt to plant the Gospel in hardened hearts. Such attempts can make the person more resistant to the Gospel. So make sure a non-Christian's heart is prepared before attempting to influence them concerning the truth of the Gospel.

Sow a variety of seed. As the saying goes, "variety is the spice of life." So when sowing the seeds of the Gospel in the hearts of non-Christians, be creative and use a diversity of approaches. Don't just give a non-Christian challenging Christian books to read; also give him Christian music tapes and recordings of personal testimonies or church worship services. Take him along to Christian concerts or to see a good Christian drama. This allows the Gospel message to penetrate his heart from a number of different angles, and so heighten the likelihood that it will take root and grow.

Sow quality seed. Don't hand out tracts that were printed in the 1940s, or books that are no longer relevant to the demands of today's society. Our goal is to get the person to read, listen to, or look at what we give them. So we must use relevant, quality, and up-to-date Christian materials in sowing the seed.

Sow wisely. Sow only as much as a person can absorb. Don't overload him; otherwise we are simply wasting time and seed. However, we should also keep in mind that the Bible tells us, "Whoever sows sparingly will also reap sparingly, and whoever sows generously will also reap generously" (II Corinthians 9:6). The point is balance. Sow generously, but only to the point it can be absorbed. If a non-Christian is open to the Gospel, sow the seed regularly and consistently into his life.

Sow compatible seed. Give a person resources that are compatible with his interests. If the person likes contemporary rock music, don't give him a southern Gospel music tape to listen to. Find the tapes of some good contemporary Christian artists to share with the person. Or if a person is a sports fanatic, give him a book by a top coach or professional athlete who is a Christian.

Watering the Seed

Once the seed is planted, it needs to be watered. The watering process begins when a non-Christian is introduced to the life of the church body—its members, activities, and worship. Whether a person takes root and grows as a Christian after his decision to receive Jesus Christ as Lord and Savior depends greatly upon watering the seed.

Church growth research tells us that the first month is critical for a person after he comes to Christ. If he is to become a mature and growing member of the church body, he must immediately develop meaningful relationships with several Christians other than the person who initially led him to Christ.[16]

In order for a person to become a faithful and growing disciple of Jesus Christ, he must become fully assimilated into the life of a good church fellowship. A missionary to Turkey told me that one of the most difficult obstacles he's had to overcome is that there is no vibrant Turkish church in which a seeking Turk can experience culturally relevant Christian teaching and worship.

Harvesting the Crops

Harvesting occurs when a Christian persuasively invites a non-Christian to believe in and receive Jesus Christ. Harvesting is the aim of the first three steps in evangelism. Our eyes must always be focused on the harvest!

Church growth expert Peter Wagner put it this way: "Farming is enjoyable. I come from a farming background and believe it is one of the most rewarding professions. But enjoyable as farming might be, professional farmers evaluate everything they do by whether a given activity contributes to the harvest. They prepare the ground and sow the seed not as an enjoyable end in itself, but as a step toward the harvest. They dig out weeds and build fences as protection against predators in order to increase the harvest. They walk through their fields in such a way as not to jeopardize the harvest. Then, when the crop is mature, they gather it in with great care in order to maximize the yield."[17]

Not every non-Christian is ripe for harvest. Those who are ready can usually be recognized by the following characteristics in their lives:

- They are open to Christian friends.

- They are not hindered by their religious background or past experiences.

- They verbally share about their personal hurts, concerns, and needs.

- They are aware that the Gospel may offer solutions to their life.

- They are verbal about their spiritual journey.

- They ask thoughtful questions about Jesus and the Christian life.

- They are willing to expose themselves to Christian activities and events.

It is important to remember the difference between persuasion and manipulation. Keep in mind that biblical persuasion has an ethical base, while manipulation does not.

"For the appeal we make does not spring from error or impure motives, nor are we trying to trick you. On the contrary, we speak as men approved by God to be entrusted with the gospel..." (I Thessalonians 2:3-4). "...We have renounced secret and shameful ways; we do not use deception, nor do we distort the word of God. On the contrary, by setting forth the truth plainly we commend ourselves to every man's conscience in the sight of God" (II Corinthians 4:2).

We are called to persuade, not manipulate. And remember, if we manipulate someone into becoming a Christian, someone else can just as easily manipulate them out of it. Our primary aim is for a non-Christian to make a willful response to accept and live for Jesus as their Savior and Lord through the agency of the Holy Spirit.

Storing the Harvest

Some conclude their discussion concerning the stages of evangelism with the concept of harvesting. This is because their evangelistic focus is to solicit decisions, not to make disciples. However, as I have pointed out, our commission is to make more and better disciples. For this reason, I personally emphasize the importance of another step in the evangelism process—that of storing the harvest.

No successful farmer would harvest a crop and

then leave it to rot in the fields. He gathers it in and stores it in a granary where it will be properly preserved and kept. Likewise, once a person becomes a Christian they must be assimilated into a local church fellowship.

Too many of us think the job of evangelism is completed once a non-Christian has made a decision to receive Jesus Christ as their personal Savior. As a result, many newly born-again Christians remain undernourished, and are never properly incorporated into the life of the Church, where they can grow and mature.

I would say we should not number a person as a true disciple or follower of Christ until he becomes an active and growing member of a local church body. It is our job as faithful witnesses to make sure that happens.

This chapter has emphasized the necessity to make disciples rather than to solicit decisions. We have looked at the process of conversion in rather abstract terms up to this point. However, conversion is not an abstract process, but one that is real and played out daily in the hearts of nonbelievers.

The purpose of this chapter has been to orient us to the reality of that process. In summary, I have placed the three previous diagrams together to help us visualize how the various aspects of the conversion process relate to one another (see Diagram Four). Before moving on to the next chapter, review these diagrams until you clearly understand the process of disciple-making.

The Conversion Process

Conversion Stages

-8	-7	-6	-5	-4	-3	-2	-1	0	+1	+2	+3
Pre-evangelism Formation						Born-again Event			Assimilation Discipleship		

People Categories

Left-end People		Middle People		Right-end People	
Hostile	Resistant	Indifferent	Interested	Receptive	Producers

Evangelism Activities

1	2	3	4	5
Cultivating	Sowing	Watering	Harvesting	Storing

Chapter Five

Understanding Oikos

I'm like many pastors. In trying to motivate my congregation to become more involved in witnessing, I've drawn attention to the effort that Mormons and other cults invest in their witnessing programs. Somehow I thought the comparison might inspire the congregation into putting more energy and time into our church's witnessing efforts.

But I no longer do this. A friend told me that for approximately every thousand doors a young enthusiastic Mormon missionary knocks on, he is invited into only one home. Once informed of this, I could not continue to use such an ineffective model to motivate the church into action.

Since then I have come across some enlightening statistics.[18] When several thousand Christians were asked what or who was primarily responsible for their conversion to Christ, this is what they said:

Evangelistic crusade	.5%
Visitation	1-2%
Special need	1-2%
Walk-in	2-3%
Church program	2-3%
Sunday school	4-5%
Pastor	5-6%
Friend/relative	75-90%

For all the resources the Church puts into evangelistic crusades, visitation programs, and the like,

the vast majority of us come to know Jesus Christ
personally through the witness of a friend or family
member. As a result, friendship evangelism is the
witnessing approach with which some pastors encourage their congregation to become involved.

However, many pastors still have a bias toward
emphasizing those witnessing methods that target
strangers with the Gospel. With little evaluation,
they often channel the church's evangelistic energy
into impersonal methods. We must all awaken to the
fact that God created us to be social beings. We were
created for relationship—relationship with God and
with one another. We should not be surprised when
we discover that the most effective avenue of evangelism is through meaningful relationships.

Our Relational Network

When we think about Jesus' style of evangelism,
we immediately think of the woman at the well or
the woman caught in adultery. However, these were
only fleeting encounters with Jesus. His main evangelistic target was His disciples. He developed intimate relationships with them. He became their
friend, and slowly—precept upon precept—He led
them to a place where they recognized Him as a
teacher, then the Messiah, and finally their Lord.

Beyond the Twelve there was another circle of 72
disciples whom Jesus sent out to do evangelistic
work (Luke 10:1-20). These were people with whom
Jesus didn't have the same depth of relationship as
He did the Twelve, but He nonetheless knew, befriended, and taught them.

When we first read the New Testament, we might
not notice this broader circle of disciples, but they
are important. Jesus built around Himself a relational network of followers. In this network, Jesus
shared the message of who He was, why He had
come, and how people should live and relate to each

other in a way that would please and glorify God.

Reading on through the Gospels into the book of Acts, we discover that the Gospel in the early Church largely spread through *relational networks*.

Acts 10 records how one of these relational networks was penetrated with the Gospel message. The story of Cornelius and his household is probably well known to many of us, and it marks a departure.

Until this time, the apostles had concentrated on winning Jews to Christ. But God's plan of redemption was bigger than the Jews; it was for all mankind. Thus God sovereignly intervened to broaden the vision and understanding of the early Church. As a result, the story of Cornelius is the point where the Gospel was first actively shared with Gentiles.

Cornelius, a centurion in the Italian Regiment, was a devout and God-fearing man. One afternoon he received a vision from God in which he was told to send messengers to Joppa and bring back the apostle Peter. At about the same time, God had also given Peter a vision in which He overcame Peter's resistance to share the Gospel with non-Jews.

Peter went to Cornelius' home and preached the good news concerning Jesus. As he preached, the presence of the Holy Spirit came upon all who heard and Cornelius and his household were saved and baptized.

Now this word translated as *household* in our English Bible is actually *oikos* in the original Greek text. Today, when we hear the word *household*, we think of the nuclear family—Mom, Dad, and the kids, all living together in the same house. But that was not its explicit meaning in the Greco-Roman world of New Testament times.

In those days your household—or *oikos*—was a much wider group of people, wider even than what we would call an extended family. Your *oikos* would certainly have included your parents, grandparents, and other blood relatives, but it would also have included friends, neighbors, and other associates. Basically, your *oikos* consisted of those people with whom you had a regular degree of relationship. It was your relational network.

When Cornelius' household was baptized, we are talking about his relational network being baptized, not just his immediate family. And we know this is true because Acts 10:24 tell us, "...Cornelius was expecting them [Peter and the messengers] and had called together his relatives and close friends." Thus, when Peter went into the house, he "found a large gathering of people" (verse 27).

In Acts 16:13-15, after Lydia had heard Paul preach, she believed and was baptized with all her household (*oikos*).

Likewise, when the Philippian jailer was converted, a similar occurrence happened. The jailer asked, "'Sirs, what must I do to be saved?' They replied, 'Believe in the Lord Jesus, and you will be saved—you and your household [*oikos*].' Then they spoke the word of the Lord to him and to all the others in his house [*oikos*]" (Acts 16:30-32).

Aristides was a post New Testament writer. He lived in the city of Athens and wrote the earliest surviving apology for Christianity, which he addressed to the emperor Hadrian in A.D. 125. Speaking about how Christians related to their households he wrote: "As for their servants or handmaids, or their children, if any of them have such, they persuade them to become Christians for the love that they have towards them; and when they have become Christians they call them without distinction 'Brothers'."[19]

From these examples we clearly see that the Gospel spread rapidly, and the Church began to grow from Jerusalem to Asia Minor and finally into Europe through the natural relationships of the *oikos*. It was to others within their *oikos* that individuals looked to discover their meaning in life. When the Gospel touched a person's life, its power spread quickly through an intimate web of relationships.

Western culture tends to emphasize the individual rather than *oikos* relationships. People often isolate themselves from each other. Yet, be that as it may, each one of us has his own *oikos* (relational network), consisting not only of immediate family members, but also of friends, neighbors, co-workers, and those with whom we socialize. The actual size of our *oikos* may vary, depending upon the opportunities we have to interact with other people and the level of social skills we have acquired. What is important to understand, however, is that we are all a part of an *oikos*, however large or small it may be.

Salt or Salt Shakers

While reaching non-Christians with the Gospel message through our *oikos* relationships is one of the most natural means of evangelism, an interesting paradox frequently occurs in our lives.

As I have shared this idea of relational networks with Christians and have encouraged them to evangelize their *oikos*, many have been surprised at how few non-Christians were within their *oikos*. The longer a person is a Christian, the fewer the number of meaningful relationships they usually have with non-Christians. It is not uncommon for some of us to have no nonbelievers within our *oikos* at all.

In his book *Bringin' 'Em Back Alive*, Danny Lehmann elaborates on this point when he states that younger Christians seem to be more effective witnesses than those of us who have been Christians a long time. He attributes this to the fact that "they haven't become so immersed in the Christian culture that they are alienated from the world, they still have unsaved friends."[20]

Jesus tells us that as Christians we are the "salt of the earth" (Matthew 5:13). This means that the Gospel message can righteously affect people and the society around us, just as salt preserves and enhances the flavor of food. If, however, we do not faithfully share the Gospel message with those around us, then we are nothing more than beautifully decorated salt shakers. And salt shakers that do not dispense salt have very little use, regardless of how beautiful they may be.

While the New Testament stresses the importance of Christians meeting together for prayer, worship, and fellowship, we shouldn't forget that we're agents of God's love to a lost and dying world, not just corporately but also individually. God has given each of us an *oikos* as our personal mission field.

It may sound extreme to some, but God may actually prefer that we attend a craft night hosted by our local school or become a member of a sports club, rather than join the church choir. In one way or another, we must be creative and put ourselves in positions where we rub shoulders with those who need to hear the message of God's love.

The thought of doing something like joining a social club or attending a sports event where we will interact with nonbelievers scares some of us. This is not necessarily because we are self-righteous or lack compassion, but because over the course of time we have lost touch with non-Christians and the world in which we live. Usually we are afraid that we will have nothing in common with a non-Christian and consequently be unable to communicate with him.

One of the best ways to overcome our fear is to rediscover the biblical truth that non-Christians are individuals created in God's image and in a lot of ways, are just like us. Once you begin developing friendships with non-Christians, you will be surprised at how much you have in common with them.

Our first step toward being an effective witness for God is to make a deliberate effort to deepen our relationships with those nonbelievers who are presently casual acquaintances. Second, we can voluntarily choose to put ourselves in places where we will become personally acquainted with other non-Christians, thus increasing their number within our *oikos*.

Now that we understand that most people come to know the Lord Jesus Christ through their relational network, we are ready to begin to reach our own *oikos* with the Gospel. The next chapter provides some practical guidance on how to begin doing this immediately.

Chapter Six

Affecting Our Oikos

It must have been quite a sight: 2,000 pigs rushed down the hillside and leaped off a cliff, only to drown in the Sea of Galilee. It certainly scared those who had been watching over the pigs. They scurried to the nearby villages to tell people about it.

People came running from all over to see for themselves. When they arrived, they were astounded to find Jesus befriending the man they all knew as an uncontrollable menace. But here he was, in his right mind and talking to Jesus.

"He cast demons out of him! He commanded the demons to go into the swine!" Comments rippled through the crowd. Nothing like this had ever happened in the land of the Gerasenes, and they were so overcome by fear that they told Jesus to go away.

As Jesus climbed into His boat to leave, the man who had been demonized asked if he could go along. Jesus replied, "Go home to your family and tell them how much the Lord has done for you."

It was a simple and straightforward commission. Jesus didn't tell the man to go the marketplace and preach the Gospel, but to go to his family and tell them how much the Lord had done for him.

"As you know, I was demonized and out of control. But I have been touched by the power of God! He has changed my life and set me free. I can now sit here in my right mind and tell you what God has done for me." It was as simple as this testimony. And we know the man obeyed Jesus and witnessed

to his family, because Scripture tells us that "all the
people were amazed" (Mark 5:20). As a result, I
believe a number of his friends and family came to
believe that Jesus was the Messiah.

The Samaritan woman whom Jesus met while
resting by Jacob's well did the same thing. She told
her entire village about meeting Jesus, and we are
told that many people believed in Jesus as a result
(John 4:39).

As I pointed out in the previous chapter, sharing
the Gospel message with relational networks became the primary way the Gospel was spread during
the early centuries of the Church. Respected theolo-
gian and historian J. G. Davies wrote, "There was no
elaborate missionary machinery; the faith was
spread rather by personal contact and example.
Hence Justin[21] could refer to many who have
'changed their violent and tyrannical disposition,
being overcome either by the constancy which they
have witnessed in the lives of their Christian neigh-
bours, or by the extraordinary forbearance they have
observed in their Christian fellow-travellers when
defrauded, and by the honesty of those believers
with whom they have transacted business.'"[22]

This relational style of evangelism, which was so
fundamental during the Church's formative years,
must once again become an important part of the
Church's evangelistic strategy. We need to begin taking relational networks seriously as God's chosen
mission field.

Instead of drawing Christians away from the
non-Christians in their *oikos* group, the Church
needs to begin encouraging and equipping them to
draw closer. We are not to isolate ourselves from
unbelievers, but to embrace them as Jesus did. God
has put each of us in a relational network so we
might model the life of Jesus for them to see.

Getting Started

Before setting out prematurely to affect our *oikos* with the Gospel, there are several practical things we should do.

Identify and list your *oikos* members.

Before we can reach out effectively to a group of people, we must know who they are. Thus we need to identify our *oikos* carefully. Our *oikos* will consist of people of common kinship (extended family), common friendship (friends and neighbors), and common associates (marketplace, clubs, school, recreation). You can use the following diagram to help you visualize your *oikos* relationships.[23]

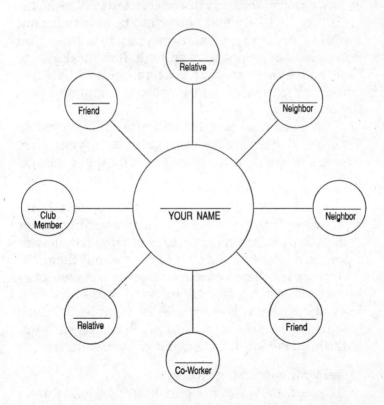

Obviously our *oikos* could end up being a very large group of people. It's helpful to identify those who are part of our *oikos* as those people with whom we spend at least one hour per week. This can be an accumulation of shorter times, but it must be a consistent time of face-to-face contact.

Write down the names of those who make up your *oikos*. With this list of names in hand, you are ready for the next step.

Write a personal profile of your *oikos* members.

Take the name of each person listed as *oikos* members and write a personal profile on them—highlight their unique interests, hobbies, and beliefs, as well as any particular needs or concerns they may have.

It is quite likely that you won't be able to fill out a profile on every person on your list, since you don't know everyone well enough. It may take some time and effort on your part to get to know the person a little better before you can complete a profile on them.

These personal profiles will prove an invaluable resource in identifying those people in your *oikos* who are probably most open to the Gospel message.

Pray over your *oikos* members.

Armed with the information of the personal profiles, we can pray intelligently and specifically for people. If there are special needs or circumstances in a person's life, then we should pray about them.

Prayer is where compassion grows. As we pray for people in our *oikos*, we begin to sense how God feels about them. He loves them completely. Such love can only constrain us to reach out to our *oikos* with the same kind of love and compassion.

Target your witnessing efforts.

If you discover that a person in your *oikos* has a need in a particular area, try to meet that need. In so doing, you will win their confidence and gain an opening to share the Gospel. Most likely, some in your *oikos* have similar interests to yours. Invite them to do something with you, where you can share your mutual interest while deepening and strengthening your relationship. Start with those you feel are most receptive to the Gospel, but don't neglect those who may be antagonistic toward it. Look over the profiles of those who are resistant. Pray for them and ask God to give you a special strategy for reaching them with the Gospel.

As human beings, we were created to relate to and depend upon one another. Friendship or companionship is a fundamental human need; if it were not so, solitary confinement would not be considered punishment. Even the most hardened and isolated person in our *oikos* needs to know that they have a friend. We can use this basic human need as a bridge across which to carry the Gospel to people who have otherwise cut themselves off from it.

It is important to remember that each person in your *oikos* also has his own *oikos*. By touching his life with the Gospel, we are in turn touching many other people in an evangelistic process that goes on like ever-widening ripples on the surface of a lake.

Small Group Partnerships

We are not called to be "witnessing Lone Rangers." Our Lord's witnessing commission was not simply given to us individually. It is a corporate call to the whole Church. There will never again be a perfect witness like Jesus who was uniquely filled with God's grace and truth (John 1:14). No single individual will possess the complete revelation and attributes of God as Jesus did. As individual Christians, we need each other. We are more effective in our witnessing endeavors when we unite our individual efforts with others.

When affecting our *oikos* with the Gospel, we must not neglect the principle of strength through cooperation. One of the best ways I know of pulling together to reach our relational networks is through the dynamics of a *small group.*

The concept of small groups of believers meeting together in someone's home has a long and noble history that goes all the way back to the foundations of the Church. In the last few decades there has been a tremendous upsurge in popularity in the use of small groups as the infrastructure of church life.[24] While many of these small groups are centered around Bible study, prayer, and fellowship, they must also become effective units for evangelism. Following is a list of several advantages which come through cooperating in evangelism through small groups.

We find mutual agreement.

Within the small group environment, we can join with other Christians and together, mutually and willfully, decide to grow in our faith and affect the world around us. We can be "one in spirit and purpose" (Philippians 2:2).

One specific spiritual discipline which is greatly enhanced through partnership is prayer. The power of prayer is multiplied when a group of Christians agrees to pray for the same need (Matthew 18:19-20). Through partnership, intercessory prayer networks or chains can be started through which we can pray for specific people in our relational networks.

We find support and encouragement.

Living as we do in a world that for the most part is resistant to the Gospel, it is inevitable that we will face rejection. However, within the confines of a small group we can receive from other Christians the personal support and encouragement we each need to combat rejection. In the small group setting, we are accepted and built up by the love and concern demonstrated for one another. The variety of "one-another" ministries required for healthy church life flourishes within a small group network.

The early Christians were also fearful of rejection. In response to their real feelings, they often prayed for God's supernatural boldness and confidence, and got it! The results were amazing: "After they prayed, the place where they were meeting was shaken. And they were all filled with the Holy Spirit and spoke the word of God boldly" (Acts 4:31).

Boldness is not being obnoxious and outspoken with others. Instead, it is discovering the empowerment which comes from being filled with the Holy Spirit, and the intimate support of Christians dwelling in unity.

We find accountability and protection.

Not one of us is free from temptation. We each need to be accountable to others in the Body of Christ. In small group accountability, we discover God's spiritual protection and covering. Within small groups, the power of personal accountability and spiritual protection is uniquely experienced.

We find a learning environment.

The small group is a tremendous learning environment. Within it we learn how to talk naturally with others about our faith. As well, we learn from the assembled wisdom of other Christians about creative ways to reach out to our *oikos*.

Perhaps you are already part of a small group in your church. If you are not, then I encourage you to band together with other like-minded Christians and start your own small group. You will find the support of such a group spiritually rewarding.

But the value of a small group is not only found in the support it can give us. The small group environment is also a wonderful setting in which to introduce members of our *oikos* to other Christians and to church life. We talked in Chapter One about the inadequacies of front-door evangelism, and the grim statistics of people who come to a church service only to be put off by the non-relational environment of a large group setting. The small group does not suffer from this same weakness.[25]

A small group is informal and comfortable. It is where individual and group evangelistic efforts merge naturally. It is a secure, non-threatening environment into which we can enthusiastically invite members of our *oikos*. In an intimate small group, nonbelievers can see the character of Christ modeled in a more natural setting. It is also the best entry point for a person to make the transition into the life of the Church—such as Sunday worship services.

The effectiveness of small groups as units of evangelism is not simply abstract theory—it is fact. The largest church in the world, Yoido Full Gospel Church in Seoul, Korea has grown to its present size of 700,000 through the multiplication of evangelistic small groups scattered throughout the city.[26]

People within our *Oikos*

Our modern society is complicated and multi-faceted. Simply because we live in the United States does not mean we partake of a homogeneous culture. Modern America is a mosaic of assorted cultures and ethnic groups. We often live side by side, yet have little understanding of one another.

In light of this fact, there will certainly be some people in our *oikos* who are from a cultural background different from our own. To reach them with the Gospel, we must enter their world. This may take some effort on our part in studying their culture and in learning to share the Gospel in ways which are sensitive and relevant. However, this is the price we must pay to witness cross-culturally.

The New Age movement is much in vogue today, and chances are we will also encounter some New Agers within our relational network. The New Age is a wide-ranging and eclectic hodgepodge of psychic and Eastern religious practices. To be effective in witnessing to New Agers, we will have to take the time to read and research more thoroughly to understand the New Age movement.

Then there are the cults. These range from Eastern religious cults like the Hare Krishna and the Divine Light Mission to pseudo-Christian cults such as Mormonism and Jehovah's Witnesses. The advent of the New Age has made the distinction between cults and the New Age fuzzy; nevertheless, we all know when we have met someone from a cult.

Again, it is quite possible that there will be people affiliated with different cults in our *oikos*. When we encounter them, many of us are unprepared and poorly equipped to witness effectively. As a result, we tend to avoid cult members. But the Gospel message is for all people, including cult members. We need to learn how to reach out to them in a loving and caring way that does not alienate them.

The following chapters are geared toward dealing with these special people groups. My purpose is information, not formula. You will not find any pat answers to give to cult members or New Agers. You will find no surefire Gospel presentation which will cross all cultural barriers. But armed with the information contained in the following chapters, you will be better prepared to relate more effectively to these people in a loving and caring way.

I have also included a chapter on witnessing in the workplace. Much of our time is spent at work, and many of the people in our *oikos* are fellow employees. A chapter on witnessing in this environment is both appropriate and strategic.

Chapter Seven

Witnessing in the Workplace

"I really envy you, involved in God's work every day. It must be wonderful not to get caught up in secular pursuits." "I wish I could serve God full time like you do. So much of my day is taken up with mundane, secular activities." As a pastor, I have lost count of the number of times comments like these have been made to me.

Implicit in such statements is the idea that to be useful and effective as a witness for Christ, we must be involved in some kind of "full-time" Christian service. Undoubtedly some of us have this specialized calling and are ministering in this area. However, the crux of the issue is, are we faithfully serving God in the place where He presently has us?

It is a crippling fallacy to draw a distinction in our daily activities between the *spiritual* and the *secular*. In allowing ourselves to do this, we will feel frustrated and unfulfilled because so much of our lives are spent in so-called secular activities. And perhaps the main secular activity in which we are involved is our work.

Over 100 million people in the United States spend at least 50 percent of their weekday waking hours at work. Multiplied millions of Christians are represented in this group. Does God, in His infinite wisdom and economy, really intend all those hours spent at work to be unproductive for the Kingdom of God? I don't believe He does. Paul wrote from prison to the Colossian Christians, "Be wise in the way you act toward outsiders; make the most of every opportunity" (Colossians 4:5).

In not having a full-time Christian position, you are in good company! Throughout the Bible, we see God using men and woman who were not professional religious workers to accomplish great things for Him. Moses was a shepherd when God appeared to him in a burning bush. David also was a shepherd, Joseph was a political leader in Egypt, and Nehemiah was the king's cup bearer. Jesus avoided aligning Himself with the organized religious leaders of His day, and instead recruited fishermen and a tax collector to share in His ministry.

We are each called to minister faithfully to those around us, whether we find ourselves in a Christian or non-Christian environment. "We are therefore Christ's ambassadors, as though God were making his appeal through us" (II Corinthians 5:20).

Wherever we are, we are called to be full-time witnesses of God's grace. The workplace is God's tailor-made mission field for many of us. It is among those in our workplace that He has commissioned us to spread His Gospel.

In your workplace, you are in a unique position. You have the opportunity to socialize daily with many different types of people—from atheists to those who are hurting and questioning the meaning of life. It would take a full-time Christian worker much time and effort to accumulate those same kinds of personal contacts. But God has placed *you* alongside these people on a daily basis.

Actions Speak Louder than Words

There are two distinct areas to consider in relation to witnessing at work. The first is how we perform our jobs; the second is the opportunities we have to be a godly influence on our co-workers.

"Slaves, obey your earthly masters in everything; and do it, not only when their eye is on you and to win their favor, but with sincerity of heart and reverence for the Lord. Whatever you do, work at it with all your heart, as working for the Lord, not for men, since you know that you will receive an inheritance from the Lord as a reward..." (Colossians 3:22-24). Here Paul tells slaves (workers) that they must not serve only when they are being watched, but that they should work faithfully for their masters (employers) at all times.

Our work performance should flow from a sincere desire to serve God. Paul indicated that when a slave carried a sack of wheat diligently for his master, in a very real sense he was also working for the Lord, and would receive a reward from Him.

In light of this, we each need to ask ourselves, "How do I work? Am I a productive employee?" Too many workers only seem committed to their job when the boss is looking. They only care about the quality of the work they do when he or she is around. But as Christians, we are to do our best at all times, motivated by the fact that we are serving God first, then our employer.

We have all heard about the Protestant work ethic which helped make the United States economically strong. This work ethic is grounded in biblical truth. Unfortunately, few of us in the workplace display any tangible evidence that we adhere to a Christian work ethic.

Before we can verbally witness to our co-workers, each of us must first ask ourselves whether we are working with all our strength, as unto the Lord. "...If anyone serves, he should do it with the strength God provides, so that in all things God may be praised through Jesus Christ..." (I Peter 4:11).

As Christian employees, we must be honest in all our dealings. Within the workplace, even Christians can be tempted to be dishonest. The workplace is often where the ethical clash of two different kingdoms—God's and man's—occurs. We may be asked by an unscrupulous employer to work more slowly to drag out a job and increase the final billing price. We may be tempted to take company possessions home. Or we may be tempted to misappropriate funds belonging to our employer. Such temptations are regular occurrences in the workplace.

As Christians, we must be unrelentingly honest in all our work situations. Once we have compromised in one area, we have given Satan a foothold in our lives, and we will soon find ourselves on a downward path where compromise in other areas of life becomes easier and easier.

To understand the emphasis God places on honesty, one can do no better than read the book of Proverbs, which has many insights for the wise: "The man of integrity walks securely, but he who takes crooked paths will be found out. Food gained by fraud tastes sweet to a man, but he ends up with a mouth full of gravel. A fortune made by a lying tongue is a fleeting vapor and a deadly snare" (Proverbs 10:9; 20:17; 21:6).

This is only a small selection of the many proverbs which refer to our relationship to work. Take the time now to pause in prayer and meditate concerning your own work habits. Does your lifestyle in the workplace please God?

Before we have the right to give advice or share the Gospel with others at work, we must be sure that we "walk our talk." Christians should be the ones who have the most credibility and respect in the workplace.

Unfortunately, this is not always the case. I recently read a grim portrayal of this point in Larry Burkett's book, *Business by the Book:*

> I recall a note I received in 1976 from the chairman of one of the largest paper companies in America. It simply said, "Thank you for the integrity you have shown in paying your bills to our company."
>
> I thought that was remarkable because our total purchases for the previous year couldn't have been ten thousand dollars—certainly only a fraction of their total sales. So I decided to call the chairman to ask why he wrote the note.
>
> He said, "Your ministry is one of the few Christian organizations we deal with that pays its bills on time—every time. I'm a Christian also, but the delinquencies among churches and other ministries has become a source of ridicule in some of our directors' meetings."[27]

Credibility and respect do not automatically accompany a position or title, but are established by the track record of our character and actions over time. It takes much time and effort to build credibility; it only takes one incident to destroy it.

"A good name is more desirable than great riches; to be esteemed is better than silver or gold" (Proverbs 22:1). As Christians, we must establish a good name and guard it well. We need to be known in the workplace as people of honesty and integrity.

Once we know for sure that we are serving in our workplace in a diligent and God-honoring way, we can seriously begin looking for opportunities to draw our co-workers closer to Christ. At first, however, this may not prove to be an easy task.

Witnessing in the Workplace

When your co-workers first learn that you are a

Christian, they may react naively by stereotyping you. This can be a painful experience for you if they have had negative encounters with Christians in the past. At times you may be ridiculed and ostracized for no apparent reason other than because you are a follower of Jesus.

The apostle Peter addresses this issue, "If you are insulted because of the name of Christ, you are blessed, for the Spirit of glory and of God rests on you. If you suffer, it should not be as a murderer or thief or any kind of criminal, or even as a meddler. However, if you suffer as a Christian, do not be ashamed, but praise God that you bear that name" (I Peter 4:14-16).

We shouldn't deliberately manifest a martyr complex and go about looking for opposition. But if the opposition is present and persists, we first want to make sure we are being "persecuted for righteousness sake," and not because of our own insensitivity or arrogance.

Our witness at work must reflect the attributes of Christ as detailed in the Sermon on the Mount (Matthew 5:1-12). We can do no better than to follow Paul's advice to Timothy in this regard. "Don't have anything to do with foolish and stupid arguments, because you know they produce quarrels. And the Lord's servant must not quarrel; instead, he must be kind to everyone, able to teach, not resentful. Those who oppose him he must gently instruct, in the hope that God will grant them repentance leading them to a knowledge of the truth" (II Timothy 2:23-25).

The message of this passage is that we should never argue with our co-workers, but should always respond in kindness and love. We must lead our fellow employees gently, one step at a time, into the ways of God. We are to avoid arguments and quarrels with them at all costs. Otherwise, we may win the argument, but lose the relationship. Such a situation has no value for us or our fellow worker.

The workplace is a competitive environment where cutthroat methods are often used to step on others on their way up the corporate ladder. There are many victims of the aggressiveness of others in the workplace, and they may feel isolated and hurt.

These are people with real needs, and we can help them in a loving and caring way. A smile, a word of encouragement, help in time of crisis—all of these register our concern as a Christian. And such acts of caring will open more doors for witnessing opportunities than anything else we do.

Praying for Our Co-workers

Last but not least, in addition to our efforts to witness in the workplace, we should pray. We should pray privately during our times of devotion, we should pray silently to ourselves while we are at work, and we should pray corporately with other Christians in our small groups or church prayer meetings. We need to became prayer warriors, contending in prayer before God for the hearts of those we are seeking to witness to.

A good motto to keep in mind with regard to prayer and witnessing is: "We need to talk to God about people before we talk to people about God."

The following points are helpful to keep in mind as we pray for our co-workers. We should pray for each person by name, asking:[28]

- That the Holy Spirit would convict them of their need for salvation.

- That the Kingdom of God would be established in your workplace and in the life of each person working there.

- That the eyes of your co-workers would be open to God's truth.

- That your co-workers would hunger for God.
- That you would find favor with your co-workers.

In his second letter to the church at Corinth, Paul likens us to a fragrant aroma spreading over all who come in contact with us (II Corinthians 2:14-15). Is that how people at work would describe us?

If we want to be effective witnesses for Christ in our workplace, then that is how our co-workers need to feel about us. And when they see us in that way, we will be able to befriend them and share the Gospel with them successfully. In a very real sense, they will already have experienced the Gospel lived out in our lives.

For further practical instruction on witnessing in the workplace, I suggest you read *Christians in the Marketplace* by Pastor Bill Hybels.[29]

Chapter Eight
Witnessing Cross-culturally

We have all seen the grainy black and white photographs of newly arrived immigrants at Ellis Island in New York. Their eyes are dark and fixed, filled with weariness, fear, and hope. They are weary from the long boat journey across the Atlantic, fearful at what lies ahead, and hopeful that the hardship and misery many had left behind in Europe was gone forever. Perhaps life in America would bring their dreams to pass.

We are a nation of immigrants! Immigration has always been a cornerstone in our nation's growth and development. Even today, record numbers of people are immigrating to the United States. And displayed in their eyes are the same hopes, fears, and weariness. But, unlike earlier waves of immigrants who crossed the Atlantic from Europe, today's immigrants are coming across the Pacific Ocean from Asia. Approximately 500,000 legal immigrants are flooding into the United States each year.

Some are poor and destitute Cambodian refugees from camps in northeast Thailand, coming in search of a new and peaceful life. Others are wealthy businessmen from Taiwan and Hong Kong, coming to further their business interests here. Thousands of international students are studying in our colleges and universities. Whatever their reasons for coming, one fact is clear: multiplied thousands of people from various ethnic and cultural backgrounds are living within the United States.

A visit to any major city quickly reveals the fact that we have become an ethnically diverse country. On almost every city block are signs in Spanish, Chinese, Japanese, and other languages we cannot decipher. Mosques, Hindu temples, and Buddhist temples are being built rapidly.

To a large degree, our cities have become microcosms of the world. For example, the Los Angeles Unified School District has identified more than 80 languages spoken in its schools. As well, 25 percent of the 600,000 children who comprise the school district have limited or no proficiency in English, and more than 50 percent of all students in the district require remedial teaching in English.

The city of Los Angeles also has the largest Mexican, Korean, Filipino, and Vietnamese metropolitan areas outside their respective countries, and the second largest Chinese and Japanese communities. Among the residents of a one-square-mile area of inner-city Chicago, 50 nations are represented.[30]

As Christians, we cannot ignore this social reality. The Bible declares, "...I looked and there before me was a great multitude that no one could count, from every nation, tribe, people and language, standing before the throne and in front of the Lamb....And they cried out in a loud voice: 'Salvation belongs to our God, who sits on the throne, and to the Lamb'" (Revelation 7:9-10).

Here John paints for us a wonderful picture of all believers standing before God and praising Him. John points out clearly that there are people from every nation, tribe, people, and language present in this heavenly congregation.

The English word *nation* is *ethnos* in Greek. This is where we get our English word *ethnic*. So these people worshiping before the throne of God are from every ethnic, tribal, people, and language group.

The Church—All Peoples

The Church is made up of all peoples! And it is a great tragedy when the Church in our country is often perceived as "white and middle class." Certainly Jesus was neither white nor middle class, and neither should His Church be. I don't mean to suggest that we should all change our identity or heritage, but we must abandon any racial and ethnic stereotyping. Only then can the Church truly become a gathering place for people from every ethnic and language group.

The best place to begin is with ourselves. We each must deal with our prejudices and stereotypes. We must become like Jesus, who allowed no ethnic or social barriers to hold Him back from ministering to *all* people. This is not to say that we shouldn't be thankful for the cultural background God has given us. However, we must be aware that our nation is a multi-cultural country, and we must embrace the cultural diversity that God has created.

One thing that can hold us back is fear. We feel comfortable and secure when we function within our own culture. We know the various cultural signals and how to respond to them, so we experience acceptance by our social group. But when we move into another culture, we are entering uncharted waters. We don't understand that culture, so we don't know how to read the cultural signals and respond to them. As a result, we often fear that we will offend others and ultimately be rejected. If left unchecked, such fear can lead to hatred, and hatred is the lifeblood of racism.

We must resist such fear. We must place our fears and concerns at the feet of Jesus, who crossed from heaven to earth in order to bring us salvation. If our

Lord could lay aside the comfort and security that
came with being at the right hand of the Father and
become a man, shouldn't we lay aside our own com-
forts and security and reach into the diverse ethnic
groups living around us?

It is likely that there will be people from different
cultural and ethnic groups in our *oikos*. Perhaps they
are fellow workers or business contacts. Perhaps
they attend our school. Perhaps they live on our
block or are members of a club we attend. Whatever
the social setting in which we know them, we must
reach out to them with the love of God.

You may ask, "How do we do this?" The first step
is simple. We must learn about and enter the culture
of the other person. This is where some common
misconceptions occur.

Common Misconceptions

There is a myth that America is a "melting pot"
of all cultures. This myth indicates that, in time, we
will flow into one another to form a homogeneous
society in which we all hold the same cultural understanding. Perhaps this was true in some measure
with earlier waves of immigrants entering our country, but it is certainly not true today.

Perhaps a better analogy would be to call America a "cultural stew." We are one country, but we are
made up of different ethnic groups. For the most
part, these groups retain the shape and color of their
own culture, much like vegetables in a stew. We can
still tell the carrots from the potatoes and beans.

Many people coming to the United States don't
find it necessary to learn English or to adapt to
mainstream American culture. Rather, they join their
ethnic brothers and sisters in communities where
they are both culturally and linguistically accepted.
For example, the 40,000 Cambodian refugees in
Southern California have settled almost exclusively

around Long Beach, and 12,000 Laotian Hmong refugees have settled in St. Paul, Minnesota.[31]

Another misconception has to do with the way we perceive our culture to be a "Christian" culture. It's common to hear a Christian say something like, "This is a Christian country. Anyone who wants to hear the Gospel can turn on a radio or television." No one can deny that the airways are saturated with Christian radio and television stations. However, that does not mean that anybody who desires to hear the Gospel can understand it.

Sadly, we have many times squeezed the Gospel into a white, middle-class mold. But many in our nation don't fit into a white or middle-class culture.

Take, for example, the Cambodian refugee population in Long Beach, California. Certainly a good number of them have televisions and radios and can easily tune into a Christian station. Unfortunately, the station is of little use to them since the majority don't speak or understand English. Those who do understand English find the message so culturally foreign that it is beyond their ability to understand and apply it to their lives.

If these people were still back in their native land, we would be sending missionaries to them. Before those missionaries were sent, they would learn the language and culture so they would be better prepared to witness cross-culturally. Simply because people from a particular ethnic group move to the United States does not mean that they have left their cultural identity behind.

The question for the Church is: Are we willing to work at overcoming our fear of relating to these different and multifaceted cultures so that they, too, may have the opportunity to receive God's Kingdom of love and joy?

As we have already mentioned, there are risks in

stepping over cultural boundaries. We may be mis-
understood and rejected. Yet we cannot allow these
obstacles to deter us.

Floyd McClung shares an example of a misunderstanding that occurred between a church in California and a group of Vietnamese refugees the church
had sponsored. The desire of the church was to see
the refugees settled with good jobs and housing.
They rallied around and reached out to the Vietnamese refugees in whatever way they could, wanting to
share Christ's love with them in a practical way,
expecting nothing in return.

But it was hard for the church not to feel a little
frustrated and used when the Vietnamese people
stopped coming to church and spurned church
members' attempts to reach out to them. This was
interpreted by the church as ungratefulness.

Thankfully, the misunderstanding was resolved
through the help of someone familiar with Southeast
Asian culture. The Vietnamese were not being un-
grateful, but had withdrawn because of the burden
of obligation they felt toward their sponsors. In their
country they were obligated to a person who showed
them kindness. Once the church understood this,
they saw a powerful analogy through which they
could share the Gospel with the refugees—we are
under no obligation to earn Christ's salvation; it is a
free gift bestowed upon us.[32]

Enter Their World

There are no quick and easy ways to witness
cross-culturally. But if we are to be successful cross-
cultural witnesses, we must be prepared to enter the
world of those with whom we desire to share the
Gospel. This may involve taking time to learn their
language, or at least to learn some common requests
and phrases in their language. It may mean going to
the library to study all we can about their culture.

It can be helpful to seek out a missionary who has served among the particular ethnic group on whom you are concentrating. Talk to the missionary and draw on his or her experience. Ask the missionary to explain the culture to you and how to relate to it. Ask about any practical tips to communicate the Gospel successfully with people in that particular culture.

And pray. Pray for sensitivity to the other culture. Pray for God's favor to be upon you. Pray that you can bridge the cultural gap that exists between you and those you desire to witness to. And finally, pray that He will prepare the hearts of those you are going to witness to.

Befriend and talk to people in that cultural group. If some of them are already part of our *oikos*, we should begin with them.

People from other ethnic groups will not be insulted if we ask them questions about their culture. Quite the opposite is true. We honor them by expressing an interest in their culture and by desiring to know more about it. So ask lots of questions. Ask how you say certain things in their language, and practice what they tell you. As you do these things, you will find a warm bond developing between you and the person from the other culture.

As your relationship develops, look for openings to share the Gospel. But always remember to share it in ways relevant to their culture. Perhaps their culture contains stories, beliefs, or practices (often called redemptive analogies) that you can use or adapt to share Gospel truth.

As you share with that cultural group, look for those who are most open to what you have to say, and focus your witnessing efforts toward them. What often happens in many tightly knit cultural groups is that once one or two make the initial decision to follow Christ, then others—sometimes the whole group—will follow their example.[33] Always be on the lookout for the most open individuals with whom to socialize.

As Christians, we have a great challenge and a great opportunity. Perhaps you have never imagined yourself leaving home to go to another country as a missionary. Well, God is doing something around us. He is bringing the world to our neighborhoods. Now we can be missionaries, learn to speak and understand a different language and culture, and never have to leave home! We can be cross-cultural witnesses right within our *oikos* and city.

God *will* have people from every ethnic, cultural, language, and people group in His heavenly Kingdom. He wants to use you and me to insure that they are there. The challenge is ours. Now is the time to reach out and begin witnessing cross-culturally.[34]

Chapter Nine

Witnessing to New Agers

One of the major problems in any discussion of the New Age movement is the difficulty in identifying any internal cohesion within it. The New Age is a decentralized movement with no recognizable or advertised central authority. It consists of a broad and bizarre spectrum of beliefs and practices dispersed throughout our society by a diverse range of individuals and organizations.

According to *Time* magazine: "The New Age does express a cloudy sort of religion, claiming vague connections with both Christianity and the major faiths of the East (New Agers like to say that Jesus spent 18 years in India absorbing Hinduism and the teachings of Buddha), plus an occasional dab of pantheism and sorcery. The underlying faith is a lack of faith in the orthodoxies of rationalism, high technology, routine living, spiritual law-and-order. Somehow, the New Agers believe, there must be some secret and mysterious shortcut or alternative path to happiness and health. And nobody ever really dies."[35]

A sampling of present New Age beliefs and practices reveals just how gullible people become when they reject historic Christianity. Read through any New Age journal, and you'll discover what the *Time* magazine article is talking about.

Following are explanations of two common beliefs in the New Age movement: rebirthing and channeling.

Rebirthing. This experience is supposed to deal with all the negative input people have received from their parents, which according to New Agers, is often the root of many of the problems they face in life. If their parents weren't very negative, perhaps the doctor who delivered them was. As they are led back through these experiences to the womb (some people go back to past lives!), they experience a rebirth in which they are set free from all the destructive influences which have hampered their lives, or so the "rebirther"—a kind of cosmic mid-wife—says. Of course, after the rebirth they usually pay the rebirther a hefty fee, which is likely to be the first negative experience of their rebirthed life.

Channeling. This is a new bent on the old occult practice of the seance. This phenomenon occurs when a medium allows a spirit to take over his mind and body. During a channeling session, the spirit's personality is shown through the medium's words, movements, speech, and the like. The medium is apparently unconscious during the session.

Perhaps the most popular entity from the "other side" on the channeling circuit today is a 35,000-year-old barbarian from the ancient lost continent of Atlantis. He has chosen to communicate the secrets of life with today's mortals through a middle-aged housewife. One wonders what relevant things a 35,000-year-old barbarian could possibly have to say about modern life.

A group in French Polynesia describes itself as "a gathering of telepathically inspired researchers, creators and spiritual adventurers living in a multidimensional paradise, preparing and realizing contacts with civilizations of the future."[36] According to this group, the earth has become disconnected from the rest of the universe. In addition, an extraterrestrial dimension continually surveys the earth.

Certain people have been chosen by these extra-terrestrials for help in restoring this rift. To aid them in this endeavor, twelve planes have been integrated into the group daily activities. These twelve planes are spiritual unification, interdimensional telepathy, poetic inspiration, awakening of the consciousness, mental structuration, emotional harmony, psychological equilibrium, regulation of vital forces, physical purification, social integration, material stabilization, and universal resonance. And people from all over the world come to be instructed by the group in these twelve planes!

While it's difficult for us to accept that people can seriously believe these things, the plain fact is that when people cut themselves loose from historic Christianity, they tend to believe in anything that sounds "spiritual," be it Eastern mysticism, occult practices, or just plain psychological hocus-pocus.

Although there is a claim of newness surrounding the varied beliefs and practices of the New Age movement, they are anything but new. The New Age movement offers a diversity of age-old, occult-based practices repackaged in contemporary guise. One former influential New Ager describes the movement as a "Satan-controlled, modern-day mass revival of occult-based philosophies and practices in both obvious and cleverly disguised forms."[37]

The New Age movement is no friend of the Judeo-Christian world view. The New Age is actively subverting it with an Eastern world view of Hinduism and neo-paganism.

New Age adherents are pursuing this goal with missionary zeal. A friend who returned home recently after spending time in Eastern Europe was greatly disturbed by the concentrated efforts he observed of New Agers trying to propagate their beliefs in that region of the world.

Uncovering the New Age Movement

New Agers come from all levels of socity. Included are influential leaders from every realm of
society—education, government, mental health,
medical, business, management, and the media.

How did the New Age come to have such a pervasive foothold in our country? Many modern Christian writers have interpreted this rise of the New
Age as the arrival of the final eschatological conspir-
acy of a one-world religion.

Such an interpretation is interesting, but the
Church must be willing to accept partial responsibility for the almost unopposed arrival of the New Age
movement in the West. As the Church began to reject
the authoritative and objective truth of the Bible, it
no longer functioned as salt and light in our society.
A secular humanist world view began to take prom-
inence, and God and the supernatural were rejected.
Humans were devalued through the teachings of
evolution and science. High technology and rationalism were said to hold the answers to the needs of
mankind. As a result, a tremendous spiritual vac-
uum was created that yearned to be satisfied.

On the heels of this came the counter-culture
movement of the 1960s and 1970s. During this time
there was a fundamental cultural shift away from the
Judeo-Christian world view of Western civilization
toward Eastern mysticism and occultism. During
this time, a preoccupation with psychedelic drugs
brought an emphasis on altered states of consciousness and the perception of ultimate reality. Since
then, a drugless alternative to this experience has
been found in Eastern mystical practices like Zen
Buddhism and Transcendental Meditation.

From these roots, the New Age movement has
arisen to fill the spiritual void with promises of
ultimate cosmic consciousness.

What Do New Agers Believe?

Since the New Age movement is such a varied collection of beliefs, fads, and rituals, it is often hard to define exactly what a New Ager believes. Instead, it is easier to define what they don't believe.

New Agers do not believe in the biblical Jesus as the *only* One who can redeem man from his sin.[38] The New Age movement claims that Jesus is one of many enlightened masters or gurus who have appeared throughout history. Jesus is recognized as someone who evolved into the highest spiritual consciousness, something for which all people should strive. Jesus was simply one "christ" among many in the spiritual hall of fame, with such enlightened ones as Buddha and Krishna.

Nor do New Agers believe in a personal God. Instead, they define God as an impersonal cosmic force or energy. In their world view there is no distinction or discontinuity between God and the cosmos or creation. Thus God cannot be known personally. One New Age motto is, "All is one."

Instead of salvation through Jesus Christ, New Agers seek it through personal enlightenment. As a person taps into cosmic consciousness through the different spiritual practices and techniques such as meditation, yoga, channeling, astrology, witchcraft, and the like, they will evolve in their own personal "godness" or oneness with the universe.

New Agers don't believe in heaven or hell, but replace them with reincarnation—a person's spirit evolves to godness through rebirth until they achieve the highest level of "christ consciousness."

Perhaps most dangerous of all, New Agers do not recognize an absolute or universal morality. The ethics of the New Age are established by each individual. Since New Agers believe that everyone partakes of godness, then almost anything is permissible.

There is no clear distinction between good and evil.

New Agers do believe in a new world order. They believe a new age is dawning in the universe: the new age of enlightenment, or the mythical Age of Aquarius, as popularized in the musical *Hair*. The exact time this new age will actually begin is difficult to predict, but many of them believe a coming messiah will bring about a new world order which comprises a new world government and religion. Some New Agers see this future one-world religion united under the banner of the New Age movement.

At the center of the New Age world view is spiritual humanism or the deification of man. The New Age movement manifests extreme self-centeredness, self-glorification, and plain selfishness.

Communicating with New Agers

After reading all this information, it is easy to become pessimistic about witnessing to New Agers. However, whatever their reasons for involvement in the New Age movement, the fact remains that these people are on a spiritual search for truth and reality. New Agers are not our enemy. More often than not, they are genuine people. It is important for us to distinguish between the religious institution of the New Age and the people involved in it.

There is a growing paranoia developing in the Church toward the New Age movement. If we fail to make the above distinction, we will find ourselves despising and condemning those active in the New Age instead of seeing them as seekers of a spiritual experience, worthy of Christ's love, and desperately in need of the Gospel.

In witnessing to someone involved in the New Age movement, it is imperative that we be informed and educated about the basic elements of the New Age world view. Any New Age believer to whom we talk will have a keen interest in spiritual things. It is to our advantage to know generally what they sub-scribe to in their beliefs. The books *Unmasking the New Age* by Douglas R. Groothuis and *Out on a Bro-ken Limb* by F. LaGard Smith are very helpful in this regard.[39] Smith's book is a scholarly rebuttal to Shir-ley MacLaine's book, *Out on a Limb*, which has be-come somewhat of a New Age bible.

As we will see in the next chapter, the major obstacle in witnessing to members of the New Age movement is the person of Jesus Christ. Unfortu-nately for New Agers, Christ's teachings do not fit into their system of "enlightened thought." Jesus said, "I am the way and the truth and the life. No one comes to the Father except through me" (John 14:6). He left no room for alternate realities.

Nor do New Agers like to address the concept of sin. Sin is an archaic concept to them, and they see it as irrelevant to modern enlightened man. Yet, when John the Baptist saw Jesus, he announced, "Look, the Lamb of God, who takes away the sin of the world!" (John 1:29). New Agers should be compassionately challenged with such passages. They need to be prodded to honestly consider the whole life and teachings of Jesus. Much of what Jesus taught does not fit with other religions, no matter how hard people may try to synthesize them. Those involved in the New Age must be asked the same question Jesus asked of Peter, "Who do *you* say I am?" (Mat-thew 16:15, italics mine).

In the course of any discussion with a New Ager, it is important to define exactly what we mean by the word *Christian*. In the confused and ambiguous world of the New Age, even the word *Christian* has been emptied of its historic meaning. This was made clear to me recently as I listened to a radio talk show. The talk show host asked listeners to call in so she could put them in touch with a woman who was, in her words, "a tremendous psychic and a wonderful Christian." We must be careful to point out to New Agers the contradiction of such thinking.

The New Age is subtle and seductive. As we mentioned, it is rooted in self-deification and pride. When witnessing to New Agers, we must be sure to remain spiritually dependent upon God. The New Age's subtle appeal to self can be an overpowering temptation. In his letter to the Galatians, Paul said, "Brothers, if someone is caught in a sin, you who are spiritual should restore him gently. But watch yourself, or you also may be tempted" (Galatians 6:1).

Regarding this, former New Age leader Randall Baer writes: "The powerful experiences and elegant philosophies in the New Age can be so utterly convincing to even the most well-intentioned persons. This is what is so sad about so many people involved in the New Age."[40] We must recognize that in the New Age movement we are not just dealing with human philosophies, but demonic powers. The New Age is nothing more than Satan masquerading "as an angel of light" (II Corinthians 11:14), and we must remain spiritually alert.

Once a New Ager professes Jesus as their Savior and Lord and repents, it is first important for them to destroy all their New Age paraphernalia (crystals, jewelry, talismans, etc.) and literature (Acts 19:17-20). A tremendous freedom comes with this act of obedience. Second, they must get involved immediately in a caring fellowship of believers where they can be nurtured and taught the Word of God.

In Walter Martin's book *The New Age Cult*, he lists several helpful points to bear in mind when witnessing to New Agers. I recommend his book.[41] In it you will find many practical helps to guide you as you seek to affect those within your *oikos* who are involved in the New Age movement.

Chapter Ten

Witnessing to Cult Members

We have all encountered cult members. They have knocked on our doors, offered us literature, and asked to talk with us about their beliefs. Or we've been confronted in airports or on the street by devotees of the latest Eastern guru soliciting donations. As we listen to their pitch, we discover that they're eager to convince us they're from the "true" way. We soon learn that they don't believe in the deity of Jesus Christ, or that He was God incarnate, but rather they veer off on some mystical tangent.

Today, cults are as much a feature of America's religious landscape as church steeples and pipe organs. Cult expert Walter Martin, founder of The Christian Research Institute, estimated that there are about 20 million cult members in the United States who are active opponents of true biblical faith.[42]

For many of us, the proliferation of people claiming adherence to cults—either aberrations of Christianity or wholesale imports of Eastern religion—is a matter of deep concern. So we've devised a variety of ways to deal with cult members. For example, some slam their door in the face of cult members who show up at their homes, and often feel smugly justified in doing so. Other Christians seek to humiliate cult members when they encounter them on the street. In so doing, we hold back the compassion and mercy cult members so desperately need to feel.

Thousands of us pray earnestly that a relative or friend involved in a cult will come in contact with a loving and compassionate Christian. How unfortunate that so often our "Christian" response to cult members lacks love and understanding.

Certainly cult members are not always easy to witness to, and we may never ourselves actually see a cult member converted. But be encouraged: cult members do repent and follow Jesus. Through our loving, caring responses we can be a link in the process of conversion. (See Chapter Five.)

I've been told that the greatest percentage of those who leave cults do so within the first three years of joining. So we must redouble our efforts to reach out to those involved in cult organizations.

Cult members are not faceless people who deserve to be heaped with ridicule and scorn. More often than not, they are diligent seekers of truth and God. We must approach them with wisdom and discernment. Cult members need to be disarmed by the love and compassion of Christ they see flowing through our lives. If they feel comfortable with us, they are more likely to let down the mask of the cult they're hiding behind and allow us to minister to their real personal needs.

A cult member is just like any other person in need of Christ's salvation. We should invest time and energy into building positive and personal relationships with them. They are not irredeemable, tragic figures, but people just like you and me, who are able to be won to Christ through compassionate love and care.

Understanding Cults

Before we look more specifically at practical ways we can reach out to cult members with the Gospel, we need to take the time to understand what a cult is and how they function.

"For what I have received I have passed on to you as of first importance: that Christ died for our sins according to the Scriptures, that he was buried, that he was raised on the third day according to the Scriptures" (I Corinthians 15:3-4). "...Every spirit that acknowledges that Jesus Christ has come in the flesh is from God, but every spirit that does not acknowledge Jesus is not from God. This is the spirit of the antichrist, which you have heard is coming and even now is already in the world" (I John 4:2).

Together, these passages of Scripture give us a clear understanding of the central theological test for discerning true and false teaching. The central truth that will unmask false cults is their teaching concerning the *person of Jesus*. All cults deny and reject the deity of the biblical Jesus. In so doing, they dismiss or distort such revealing Bible passages as John 1:1, "In the beginning was the Word, and the Word was with God, and the Word was God."

We can respectfully disagree on many nonessential or non-redemptive issues in the Christian faith, like the exact time and manner of Christ's second coming. But we cannot disagree on vital essentials to our faith like the deity of Jesus Christ (I John 2:22-23). Neither can we leave unchallenged any individual or group rejecting the essential redemptive teaching of our faith as stated by Paul: "[We] are justified freely by his grace through the redemption that came by Christ Jesus" (Romans 3:24).

The New Testament tells us that certain teachings are inspired and empowered by demons. "The Spirit clearly says that in later times some will abandon the faith and follow deceiving spirits and things taught by demons" (I Timothy 4:1). I believe we are living in a day when doctrines of demons are being spread by false teachers and false prophets. Many people claiming to be followers of Christ are actually following teachings that suit their own preconceived ideas. Many people are turning to a "different gospel" (Galatians 1:6).

"For the time will come when men will not put up with sound doctrine. Instead, to suit their own desires, they will gather around them a great number of teachers to say what their itching ears want to hear. They will turn their ears away from the truth and turn aside to myths" (II Timothy 4:3-4).

Based upon the above passages, it is fair to say that when we encounter cultic teaching we enter into the realm of spiritual warfare against deceiving spirits of darkness. We are engaged in a spiritual battle!

Demon-inspired groups and teachings are not new. Jesus warned us to remain alert against such deception. He said that many people would even come claiming that they are the Christ (Matthew 24:4). The New Testament Church constantly challenged the cults of its day. John identified false teachers and prophets who departed from the apostle's teaching as antichrists (I John 2:18).

Whether the cult member we are witnessing to is our brother, our neighbor, or a stranger, the following points will help us in understanding what they believe, and why.

Cult members try to convince us that they are a part of the "Only True Church."

Most cult members believe themselves to be a divinely chosen group appointed by God to restore truth through their exclusive teaching. Because of this, cult members often feel they possess a superior insight and knowledge.

Cult members are asked to believe that their leaders are the only channel for truth, protection, and guidance. They see their leaders as unique mediators to God. However, Jesus Christ is the only mediator between God and man (Hebrews 12:24).

Cult members have difficulty explaining where Jesus fits into their overall theology.

The real issue between cults and the historic Christian Church is the cult's view of the person of Christ and His eternal redemptive work on the cross. When we try to clarify with cult members what they actually believe about Jesus, they often become very evasive. Usually they will give a quick answer and attempt to steer things back on to theological ground they are more sure of.

Cult members are often isolated or separated from others, either physically or psychologically.

Cult members normally feel that everyone is against them, especially Christians. This persecution complex creates a fear of outsiders. They are often taught by their leaders that Christians will try and lead them away from the "true path." This pervasive fear keeps cult members from honestly talking with us about their questions and concerns. And it is this instilled fear of the outside world which often keeps them trapped inside a cult organization for years.

Cult members pledge total allegiance to the cult.

Cults thrive on the total allegiance and submission of members to the group. Cult members may face excommunication from the group if they seriously question the teaching or practices of the cult and its leaders. It is often very difficult for them to leave a cult without experiencing some form of social and even physical persecution.

Cult members are required to live up to all rules and policies of the group, which often brings strict legalistic control over them and their families. The concerns and tasks of the cult have first priority over individuality and the family unit.

There is usually a definite hierarchy of power and influence in a cult—an inner circle and an outer circle. There is often a small elite group of leaders controlling every aspect of the lives of cult members.

Cult members are told that to manifest doubt or to question what they have been taught is wrong. They rarely think critically for themselves. As a result, it is very difficult for cult members to have a meaningful and open discussion with others about truth and God.

Cult members normally believe that not only the Bible, but other books are divinely inspired.

Most pseudo-Christian cults claim to possess a book of revealed truth which either enhances or supersedes the authority of the Bible. For example, the Latter Day Saints have the *Book of Mormon*, and Christian Scientists trust in *Science and Health*. The Jehovah's Witnesses have their own version of the Bible, *The New World Translation*, which is filled with numerous translation errors.

Most cult members believe the end of the world is imminent.

Many cults claim to have divine knowledge concerning the "end times." Some cults have even published specific dates for the world's apocalyptic end. But Jesus clearly stated that "no one knows about that day or hour" (Matthew 24:36). Often these apocalyptic declarations are used by cult leaders to keep followers under their control. If their followers believe the world is going to end in five years, they will pour their energies into the cult in preparation for the soon-to-come apocalypse. As a result of their leader's apocalyptic end-time visions, some cult groups are presently building bomb shelters and storing huge amounts of food in preparation for the cataclysmic end of the world.

Cult members constantly look for others to pull into the cult, thus validating themselves and perpetuating the cult.

Most cult groups are very zealous when it comes to proselytizing. Cult members are often taught that witnessing is a work of salvation. They are trapped in a legalistic view of faith where their salvation is dependent upon their effort at proselytizing.

Witnessing to Cult Members

God loves cult members! They are people whom Jesus died to redeem. As followers of Christ, we must reach out to them with the Gospel. There are no witnessing formulas to employ. The most import-ant thing to remember is to be open to the leading of the Holy Spirit and sensitive to the feelings of the cult member.

Following are some practical points which will be of help as you witness compassionately to those trapped in cults.

Know what you believe and why you believe it.

We Christians should not only know what we believe, but why we believe it. We must have a thor-ough knowledge of the basic Christian doctrines of the historical Church.[43] Such knowledge will help us stay on track under the barrage of Scriptures which cult members hurl at us to supposedly prove their doctrines. To address some of their arguments, we need to know the context in which these verses occur in the Bible.

While we are not called to argue, we are to stand firm in the truth. We must study and be prepared (I Peter 3:15).

Ask probing questions.

Compassionate Christians who ask cult members meaningful questions can produce witnessing fruit. The testimonies of ex-cultists confirm that their spir-itual exodus began when a loving Christian asked a penetrating question which made them think more deeply about what they believed.

We can be confident that the Holy Spirit will continue to work after we have sown the seed of the Word of God in a person's heart through the use of some probing questions.

Define your terms.

One thing that may confuse us when witnessing to cult members is a failure to define terms. Cult members often use language which is familiar to Christians. However, while the vocabulary may be the same, the meaning assigned to the words and phrases is quite different. It is important that we find out what a particular term means within the cult's overall belief system. Having discovered this, we should be prepared to use other words and phrases that will clearly convey what we believe.

Stay focused.

It is crucial that we remain focused in any discussion with a cult member. The essential question in any witnessing dialogue should revolve around the identity of Jesus. We must keep coming back to this question.

Many cult members will want to avoid the issue of Jesus, opting instead to get lost in the smoke screen of peripheral issues. The deity of Jesus is often a stumbling block to them and their belief system. We must keep the conversation centered on the person and the redemptive work of our Lord Jesus Christ.

Which Bible?

In order to witness effectively to cult members, we have to deal with the issue of their "bibles." Some like the Mormons will claim that the Christian Bible has been changed or is no longer reliable. I suggest you ask them for documentation to back up such dogmatic statements. I highly recommend the book *The New Testament Documents: Are They Reliable?* by

F.F. Bruce.[44] It's a very good resource book explaining the uniqueness and reliability of the Bible.

Most cult members are trained to use a predetermined witnessing script. Beyond the few Bible verses they distort, the average cult member is largely ignorant about the contents of the Bible.

Target the heart, not the head.

Many of us make the mistake of targeting the heads of non-Christians through rational arguments instead of targeting the spiritual condition of a person's heart. As a result, we frequently end up in an intellectual battle with non-Christians over ideas and philosophies. Such verbal exchanges usually produce sparks and heat, but little true illumination.

While there is a place for well-informed apologetics in witnessing to cult members, we must never forget that we can't argue people into the Kingdom of God. If arguments worked, the Kingdom of God would be bursting with converted cult members, since Christians usually argue with them more than with any other group of people they meet.

The Bible tells us that "the Lord's servant must not quarrel" (II Timothy 2:24). Don't allow yourself to get into an argument. It will only harden a person's heart, and serves no eternal purpose.

Once a cult member shows a willingness to receive Jesus as Savior and Lord and be delivered from the bonds of their cult, we must be there for them. This is where our small group can be of immeasurable value. Assimilating a converted cult member into a caring small group can help them pick up the pieces of their life.

As they grow in Christ, there will be many areas in which they will need a lot of patience and help. If you find someone ready to come out of a cult, it is often best to have your pastor or a trained Christian counselor help you. It is not uncommon for a converting cult member to embark upon a long journey of healing before they can find the freedom and joy in Christ that they have so earnestly sought.

There are a multitude of cult groups, and this chapter cannot provide you with all the necessary information on today's cults. For more specific information I encourage you to read *The Kingdom of the Cults* by Walter Martin, *The Lure of the Cults* by Ron Enroth, and *Another Gospel* by Dr. Ruth Tucker. Dr. Tucker is also the featured teacher in *Counterfeits by the Book*.[45]

Conclusion

In the early summer of 1974, I was sitting with hundreds of other young travelers in Amsterdam's Vondel Park. It seemed an unlikely place for someone who had recently been drafted from high school into professional baseball. I was supposed to have life by the tail; now I was searching for its meaning in the hashish-filled air of Amsterdam, Holland.

The "hippie trail" began in Amsterdam and wound its way across Europe and the Middle East before ending in the Far East, where gurus and drugs were plentiful. Like many other young travelers, I had been wandering around on the trail for several months.

As I sat in Vondel Park pondering where to go next, a young couple sat down beside me. Although they wore loose Indian-type clothing and had the long hair and earrings typical of so many on the trail, this couple was different from the others I had met along the way. A conversation soon developed, and I found myself enjoying their company. They were happy and relaxed.

As we talked, I asked them what they were doing in Amsterdam. They gave me an unexpected answer. "We live in a Christian community on two houseboats called 'The Ark,' just behind the central train station." They invited me for some tea and dinner at The Ark. I said "yes," thinking that some day when I had nothing else to do, it might be interesting to visit them.

"How about tonight?" they asked excitedly. "In fact, why don't you come with us right now?" Before I knew it, I was on a tram with my backpack, heading for The Ark.

Getting off the tram, we walked through the train station and through the back doors. We turned left and walked a block or so along the waterfront behind the station, then turned onto a pier. A neatly painted sign read, "The Ark." We had arrived.

I was immediately surprised by the community members. They looked nothing like Christians—at least not like the Christians I had known back home. They were dressed much like the couple I came with—like the rest of us on the hippie trail. I discovered later that many of them had been active travelers on the trail before becoming Christians. Several had also come from Kabul, Afghanistan, where they had been ministering to young dropouts on the eastern end of the hippie trail. I was immediately impressed by these people. They weren't stuffy, but friendly and relaxed; not hard pressing or aggressive, but hospitable.

The couple led me into a section of the houseboat called the Afghan Room. Several others joined us, and we sat cross-legged on floor pillows which surrounded a small table onto which a pot of tea was placed. Several other small groups sat talking throughout the room. It was a peaceful atmosphere, convenient for intimate conversation. Its homey atmosphere was a welcome change from street life.

As we sat drinking tea, I was on the alert. I had heard of the sly tricks used by cultic religious groups. Amsterdam was filled with a smorgasbord of cults, everything from Hare Krishnas to the Children of God. After several minutes of cautious observation, I began to feel the genuineness of this group of people.

We casually talked about my life and their Christian commitment. Even as we discussed Christianity, I didn't feel threatened. These were people with an authentic, functional faith, and they were relaxing to be around. I found myself impressed by them.

After about an hour, I followed my hosts into the dining room for dinner. As we entered, the rest of the people were sitting down at tables adorned with tablecloths, flowers, and candles. Their faces were not somber, but full of life and laughter.

Soon a large man (6-feet, 6-inches tall) with a long ponytail and beard greeted us. His name was Floyd McClung, and he was leader of the community. Still a little uneasy, I was taken by surprise when Floyd introduced me as their dinner guest. The community responded warmly by clapping. It was a welcome contrast to the impersonal ways of the hippie trail.

After prayer, designated community members served a hearty meal family-style to each table. By the time dinner was over, I knew there was something real about these people.

To make a long story short, after several weeks of mingling with these Christians, I made my first tentative steps toward following the Lord Jesus Christ, and soon became an active member of The Ark community.[46]

Looking back over my own conversion, what attracted me to the person of Jesus Christ was not words or systematized Gospel presentations. Rather, it was the practical demonstration of genuine care and concern a small group of Christians showed toward me. It was not a single individual who led me to acceptance of Jesus Christ as my Savior and Lord. A small group of spiritually dynamic Christians all played a part in the process.

That is why I have written this book. I am no different from anyone else. In Amsterdam, I was doing what we all do in life in our own way—I was searching for reality and purpose. Yes, I was a product of the turbulent years of cultural shift that occurred in our society in the late 1960s and early 1970s. But my search was real. God has created within each of us a hunger to seek spiritual reality and purpose in life.

Today, as much as at any other time, people are still searching. However, people will not find God's reality in words alone; they must have it demonstrated for them. They must see the Gospel lived out through our lives and churches.

My prayer is that we would truly have a heart for others, that we would follow the example of Jesus and become living demonstrations of the Gospel to a hurting and lonely world. If we will do this, I believe we will see an abundant harvest of people coming to accept Jesus Christ as their Lord, and serving Him within the family of God.

People long for reality, and that is what we must give them—not prepackaged words and Gospel presentations, but real lives touched and changed by the power of God.

We are the message!

Questions for Individuals and Groups

Introduction

1. Have you ever encountered a street preacher? Was your experience positive or negative? Why?

2. What does it mean when Jesus said He would make us "fishers of men"? Do you agree with the author's two-part explanation (page 16)?

3. Do you agree with the author when he states that changed lives are the ultimate goal of witnessing (page 17)? Explain your answer.

4. According to the author, on what basis should we evaluate everything we do in the service of God? Do you agree or disagree?

Chapter One: Liberated to Witness

1. Have you ever participated in a witnessing program like Victor? Did you memorize a witnessing script? Was your experience similar or different?

2. The author states that the "program mentality" of the Church is a major obstacle which must be overcome to become effective in witnessing. Do you agree or disagree? Explain your answer.

3. What is front-door evangelism?

4. What is the nature of large groups?

5. Who is the Church?

6. What is the role of apostles, prophets, evangelists,

pastors, and teachers in the Body of Christ?

7. The author calls for a liberation. What does he state that the Church must be set free from?

Chapter Two: Treasure in Jars of Clay

1. Explain the meaning of II Corinthians 4:7 as understood by the author.

2. The author gives five common misconceptions which often keep Christians from being the effective witnesses God wants them to be. Name all five. With which two can you best identify?

3. What does the author mean when he speaks about the credentials of the heart? Identify the five credentials of the heart which every witness of Christ must possess to be effective.

Chapter Three: Message or Messenger

1. What is communication breakdown?

2. What are the three essential ingredients to effective communication?

3. What percentage does each ingredient play in effective communication?

4. What does the author mean when he says Christians are both the messenger and the message?

5. What does I John 2:6 mean to you?

6. What does the author mean when he states that Jesus is the icon of God?

7. How did Jesus differ from the religious leaders of His day?

8. Did Jesus have a witnessing formula which He followed during His earthly ministry? Explain your answer.

9. What does it mean that Jesus was a friend of sinners?

10. How did Jesus have compassion for others?

11. What does the author mean when he states that Jesus was personally approachable?

12. How can we as Christians become people-centered?

13. Describe the prayer life of Jesus. How is it applicable to ours?

Chapter Four: Disciples, Not Decisions

1. The author states that Christians often confuse decisions with disciples. What does he mean? Do you agree or disagree?

2. As Great Commission Christians, what is our goal (page 52)?

3. Do you agree or disagree with Peter Wagner's definition of evangelism (page 52)? Define evangelism in your own words.

4. According to the author, when should someone be identified as a disciple of Jesus Christ?

5. Why is the Engel Scale a helpful tool for Christians?

6. Identify the three stages within the spiritual conversion process.

7. The author states that we are part of a team of Christians God uses to bring someone to Christ. What does he mean?

8. Name the three categories of people we will all encounter when sharing the Gospel. Identify some other biblical examples of each of these people categories.

9. How is the conversion process like farming? Name the five areas of evangelism identified by the author.

10. Why is cultivating the soil considered the hardest work of evangelism? Spiritually speaking, what does cultivating the soil mean?

11. Identify the five practical tips to use when sowing the Gospel message. Do you have any other suggestions to be added to this list?

12. What does watering the seed mean? According to church growth research, why is watering the seed so important?

13. What are the key characteristics of those individuals who are most ready for the harvest?

14. Why do many Christians skip over the importance of storing the harvest?

Chapter Five: Understanding *Oikos*

1. How do most people come to know Jesus Christ as Savior and Lord? What is your testimony?

2. Why did God create us?

3. According to the author, what is the most effective form of evangelism? Do you agree or disagree?

4. What is our household or relational network?

5. The author states that often the longer someone is a Christian, the fewer non-Christians they have in their relational network. Is that true for you?

6. Why does the author suggest that you might join a special club or attend a sports event instead of joining the choir?

Chapter Six: Affecting Our *Oikos*

1. What was the primary way the Gospel spread during the early centuries of the Church?

2. Identify the four beginning steps the author suggests for affecting your *oikos*. Do you have any other suggestions to be added to the list?

3. How many people are a part of your *oikos*?

4. How many of them are non-Christians?

5. What does the author mean when he says God has not called us to be "witnessing Lone Rangers"?

6. What is the best way to pull together in reaching our relational networks, according to the author?

7. What is the advantage in partnering together in evangelism through small groups?

8. How did the largest church in the world grow to its present size?

Chapter Seven: Witnessing in the Workplace

1. Explain the distinction between the spiritual and the secular?

2. Why is the workplace God's mission field for many of us?

3. Does God care how we do our work? Explain.

4. Explain the Protestant work ethic (I Peter 4:11).

5. Why is credibility and integrity so important in the workplace? Use Proverbs 22:1 in your explanation.

6. How should we treat those in the workplace who have been isolated or hurt by others?

7. What is a good motto to keep in mind with regard to prayer and witnessing?

8. Review the prayer points the author gives for praying for your fellow employees. What are some other prayer points you can add?

Chapter Eight: Witnessing Cross-culturally

1. How does Revelation 7:9-10 relate to the United States and its ethnic diversity?

2. What is the word *nation* in Greek? What does it mean?

3. How can fear stop us in cross-cultural witnessing?

4. What is the "melting pot" myth? Explain the "cultural stew" analogy.

5. What misconception do we often have about living in a "Christian" culture?

6. What does the author mean by entering someone else's world?

7. What does it mean to be culturally relevant in our witnessing efforts?

8. Name the people you know who are from a different ethnic heritage and culture than yours.

Chapter Nine: Witnessing to New Agers

1. What is one of the major difficulties in discussing the New Age movement?

2. What happens when we reject historic Christianity?

3. Does the New Age movement accept the Judeo-Christian world view? If not, which world view do they replace it with?

4. How did the New Age movement become so popular in the United States? Was the Church responsible at all?

5. Do the New Agers believe in the biblical Jesus? If not, who do they believe Jesus was?

6. Do the New Agers believe in a personal God?

7. What is reincarnation?

8. What does the author mean when he says that New Agers believe in the deification of man?

9. Are New Agers our enemies? Explain.

10. Is it important that we are informed about the New Age movement if we are going to witness effectively? Why?

11. Does Jesus' teaching about Himself fit into New Age teaching? Use John 14:6 in your explanation.

12. What should a New Ager do once he is saved?

Chapter Ten: Witnessing to Cult Members

1. What are some of the ways Christians respond to cult members? Are these biblical responses?

2. How can Christians disarm cult members?

3. What is the central theological truth which will unmask false cults?

4. What is the difference between essential and non-essential issues?

5. Why are we in a spiritual battle when we witness to cult members? Use I Timothy 4:1 in your explanation.

6. Identify the seven characteristics of cult members. Do you have any suggestions to add to the list?

7. Why is it so important to know what we believe and why we believe it?

8. Why is it so important to define our terms when witnessing to cult members?

9. Should Christians ever get into arguments with a cult member? Why? Use II Timothy 2:24 in your explanation.

10. Once a cult member receives Jesus as Savior and Lord, what steps should be taken?

Notes

1—*Gentle Persuasion*, Joseph C. Aldrich (Multnomah Press, Portland, Oregon, 1988), p. 10. Research indicates that only ten percent of believers are gifted to share Christ using the methods presented in almost 100 percent of the classes on personal evangelism.

2—*Prepare Your Church for the Future*, Carl George (Fleming H. Revell, Tarrytown, New York, 1991), p. 44. George's research reveals that 95 percent of growth in almost all significantly large churches today comes as a result of the transfer of Christians, not conversions. This book is one of the most helpful I have read in some time.

3—Ibid, p. 65.

4—*Gentle Persuasion*, Joseph Aldrich, p. 98.

5—*Your Spiritual Gifts Can Help Your Church Grow*, C. Peter Wagner (Regal Books, Ventura, California, 1979), p. 177.

6—For a detailed discussion of spiritual warfare, see *Spiritual Warfare for Every Christian*, Dean Sherman (YWAM Publishing, Seattle, Washington, 1990).

7—*Gentle Persuasion*, Joseph Aldrich, p. 60.

8—*Out of the Saltshaker*, Rebecca Manley Pippert (InterVarsity Press, Downers Grove, Illinois, 1979), p. 128.

9—*Biblical Archaeology Review*, May/June, 1992, pp.

59-60. "The classical Greek word *hypocrites*, translated into English as 'hypocrite,' primarily means stage actor, that is, one who plays a part or pretends. *Hypocrites* could also describe a person who practiced deceit."

10—*Jesus Teaches on Prayer*, Ray C. Stedman (Word Books, Waco, Texas, 1977), p. 41.

11—For detailed discussions of the popular concept of Power Evangelism, see *Christianity with Power* by Charles H. Kraft (Vine Books, Ann Arbor, Michigan, 1989) and *Power Evangelism* by John Wimber (Harper & Row, San Francisco, California, 1986).

12—*Strategies for Church Growth*, C. Peter Wagner (Regal Books, Ventura, California, 1987), p. 128. On page 130, Wagner quotes John Stott's excellent definition of evangelization: "The nature of evangelization is the communication of the Good News. The purpose of evangelization is to give individuals a valid opportunity to accept Jesus Christ. The goal of evangelization is the persuading of men and women to accept Jesus Christ as Lord and Savior, and serve Him in the fellowship of His Church."

13—Created by James Engel of Wheaton College.

14—In creating my own version of a Resistance/Receptivity diagram, I have used certain aspects of Ed Dayton's scale. See *That Everyone May Hear* (second edition), Edward R. Dayton (MARC Publications, Monrovia, California, 1980), p. 47.

15—*The Fight*, John White (InterVarsity Press, Downers Grove, Illinois, 1976), p. 73.

16—*Gentle Persuasion*, Joseph Aldrich, p. 98.

17—*Strategies for Church Growth*, C. Peter Wagner, p. 59.

18—*The Master's Plan*, Win and Charles Arn (Church Growth Press, Pasadena, California, 1987), p. 43.

19—Aristides, quoted in *The Normal Christian Birth*, David Pawson (Hodder and Stoughton, London, England, 1989), p. 176.

20—*Bringin' 'Em Back Alive*, Danny Lehmann (Whitaker House, Springdale, Pennsylvania, 1987), p. 141.

21—A Christian teacher in Rome who was an important second-century apologist for the Gospel.

22—*The Early Christian Church*, J. G. Davies (Baker Book House, Grand Rapids, Michigan, 1980), p. 87.

23—*Beyond Church Growth*, Robert E. Logan (Fleming H. Revell, Tarrytown, New York, 1989), p. 105.

24—*Prepare Your Church for the Future*, Carl George. George's book describes the "Meta-model" structure for the contemporary Church, which is organized on small or cell groups.

25—Ibid., pp. 73-74.

26—*Successful Home Cell Groups*, Dr. Paul Yonggi Cho (Bridge Publishing, Inc., South Plainfield, New Jersey, 1981).

27—*Business by the Book*, Larry Burkett (Thomas Nelson, Inc., Nashville, Tennessee, 1990), p. 23-24.

28—This prayer list was given to me by a businessman in my congregation.

29—*Christians in the Marketplace*, Bill Hybels (Victor Books, Wheaton, Illinois).

30—*Nine Worlds to Win*, Floyd McClung, Jr. and Kalafi Moala (Word Publishing [U.K.], Milton Keynes, England, 1989), p. 60.

31—Howard G. Chua-Eoan, "Strangers in Paradise," *Time* magazine, April 9, 1990, p. 32.

32—*Wholehearted,* Floyd McClung Jr. (InterVarsity Press, Downers Grove, Illinois, 1990), p. 21.

33—This missiological concept is identified as a "people movement."

34—For a detailed discussion of witnessing cross-culturally, I suggest you study *Christianity in Culture,* Charles H. Kraft (Orbis Books, Maryknoll, New York, 1987).

35—*Time* magazine, December 7, 1987, p. 64.

36—*Wellington Evening Post,* February 10, 1990.

37—*Inside the New Age Nightmare,* Randall N. Baer (Huntington House, Lafayette, Louisiana, 1989), p. 78.

38—For a detailed study, see *Revealing the New Age Jesus,* Douglas Groothuis (InterVarsity Press, Downers Grove, Illinois, 1990).

39—*Unmasking the New Age,* Douglas R. Groothuis (InterVarsity Press, Downers Grove, Illinois, 1986). *Out on a Broken Limb,* F. LaGard Smith (Harvest House Publishers, Eugene, Oregon, 1986).

40—*Inside the New Age Nightmare,* Randall Baer, p. 19.

41—*The New Age Cult,* Walter R. Martin (Bethany House Publishers, Minneapolis, Minnesota, 1989).

42—*The Kingdom of the Cults,* Walter R. Martin (Bethany House Publishers, Minneapolis, Minnesota, 1985), revised and expanded edition, p. 15.

43—*Renewal Theology, Vol. I-III,* J. Rodman Williams (Zondervan Publishing House, Grand Rapids, Michigan, 1988, 1990, 1992).

44—*The New Testament Documents: Are They Reliable?,* F.F. Bruce, M.A., D.D. (Eerdmans Publishing Company, Grand Rapids, Michigan, 1972).

45—*The Kingdom of the Cults,* Walter R. Martin (Bethany House Publishers, Minneapolis, Minnesota, 1985), revised and expanded edition. *The Lure of the Cults & New Religions,* Ronald Enroth (InterVarsity Press, Downers Grove, Illinois, 1987). *Another Gospel,* Ruth A. Tucker (Zondervan Publishing House, Grand Rapids, Michigan, 1989). *Counterfeits by the Book,* David J. Gyertson, Ph.D, ed. (CBN Publishing, Virginia Beach, Virginia, 1990).

46—For more details on Floyd McClung's ministry on the hippie trail and in Amsterdam, see *Living on the Devil's Doorstep,* Floyd McClung, Jr. (Word Books, Waco, Texas, 1988).

If you would like to to discuss this material with the author or schedule him as a speaker, you may contact him at:

Kempsville Presbyterian Church
805 Kempsville Road
Virginia Beach, VA 23464

Phone (804) 495-1913
Fax (804) 495-1141